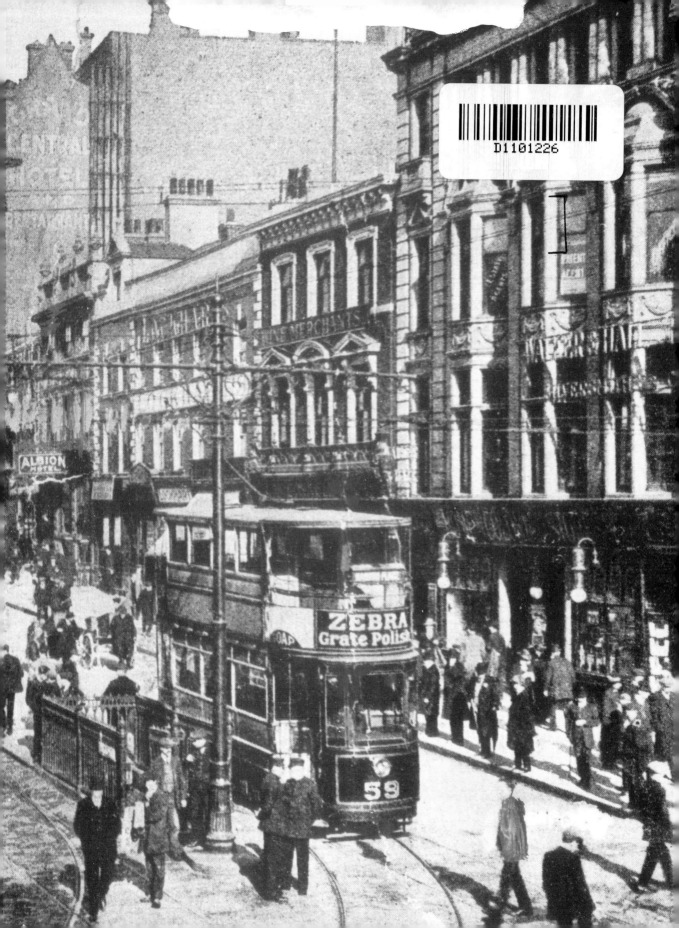

· YORKSHIRE ALBUM ·

Photographs of Everyday Life 1900–1950

· YORKSHIRE ALBUM ·

Photographs of Everyday Life 1900–1950

MARIE HARTLEY AND JOAN INGILBY

J.M. Dent & Sons Ltd
London

First published 1988
Text © Marie Hartley and Joan Ingilby 1988

This book is set in 11/14pt Caslon Old Face by Gee Graphics
Printed in Great Britain by Butler & Tanner Ltd, Frome and London, for
J.M. Dent & Sons Ltd
91, Clapham High Street, London SW4 7TA

British Library Cataloguing in Publication Data

Yorkshire Album: Photographs of Everyday Life 1900-1950
  1. Yorkshire – Social life and customs
  2. Pictorial works
  I. Hartley, Marie   II. Ingilby, Joan
  942. 8′1082′0222   DA670.Y6

· Contents ·

. . . our history since 1901 has been a history of successive transformation

Laslett

· *Preface and Acknowledgments* ·

The brief for this photographic album is the half century from 1900 to 1950, and the scene the whole of Yorkshire. The county had not then been mutilated by boundary changes followed by local authority re-distribution. Yorkshire was Yorkshire, the largest county in England covering 3,889,432 acres, and with the three historic divisions of the North, West and East Ridings intact. We, as writers, are old enough to have lived in Yorkshire, either in the West or the North Ridings, for a large part of the period under review. We have written many books on aspects of the county so that the knowledge gained, together with memories of a lifetime, have guided us in choosing the photographs. Many of these come from our own albums, others from those of relatives and friends, as well as from library and museum collections, so the reader may detect a sense of personal choice.

When we were beginning this book, we came by chance across the water colour by Girtin of Kirkstall Abbey painted in 1800. Fields slope down to the River Aire and rise up in the distance to Yeadon Moor. Only the abbey ruins, a farm building or two and a man on horseback enliven the scene, except that following the course of the river, smoke and a few chimneys can just be seen. This is Kirkstall Forge which has been there since 1600 and was a harbinger of things to come.

A hundred years later the stage had been set. Industries, cities and towns, their Victorian buildings blackened by soot, their streets clanging with trams, had overrun the green spaces, and many people had come to live in suburbs and overcrowded ghettoes. As a result, the outlying countryside, simultaneously losing its own industries – lead-mining, textiles, coalmining – was denuded of its craftsmen, labourers and small farmers.

The next fifty years were, however, to witness even more far-reaching change – the most dramatic since the Industrial Revolution. The period includes the two World Wars which, although devastating and horrific, marked significant social change and – particularly after the Second – global transformation. Factory,

Health, Education and Housing Acts were passed, culminating in slum clearance, a boom in house building, and the National Insurance Act of 1946 establishing the Welfare State. Above all, motorised transport and the aeroplane altered people's life styles, and as electricity replaced gas, oil lamps and candles, it revolutionised work in industry and in the home.

Yorkshire Album has been made possible by the co-operation of many friends, librarians and curators of museums who have both found photographs from their collections for us and have given us information about them. We wish to put on record our thanks and appreciation for their help. We should like to mention everyone by name, but the list would be very long, and the acknowledgments cover almost all involved.

The photographs are reproduced by courtesy of the following: Bayle Museum Trust, Bridlington, 40, 248, 249, 275, 297; Beck Isle Museum, Pickering, 3, 98, 128, 172, 254; Bradford City Art Gallery and Museums, 107; Bradford Telegraph and Argus, 216; Central Library, Middlesbrough, 73; Cusworth Hall Museum, Doncaster, 23, 114; Doncaster Museum and Art Gallery, 102, 213, 271; Green Howards Museum, Richmond, 101; Harrogate Museum and Art Gallery Service, 69, 70, 71, 72; Heckmondwyke Library, 14, 203; Hull Museums, 63; Humberside Leisure Services, 82, 229, 230, 231, 242; Langbaurgh Leisure Services, 35, 79, 118, 171, 247, 282; Leeds City Libraries, 49, 100, 104, 169, 188, 214; Leeds Civic Trust, 211; National Coal Board, 48; North Yorkshire County Library, 210; Pontefract Museum, 42; Sedbergh School, 39; Sheffield City Libraries, 62, 117; Sheffield Newspapers Ltd., 116; Terrys of York, 212; Tolson Memorial Museum, Huddersfield, 175, 181, 182, 201, 217; Wakefield Museum, 218, 219; Whitby Museum, 220; Whitby Photographic Society, 50; Wood Group, Bradford, 44, 45, 61, 105, 106, 156, 204, 207, 262, 294, 298; Yorkshire Air Museum, Elvington, York, 103; Yorkshire Archaeological Society, 80, 215, 219, 261, 265; Yorkshire Area: National Union of Mineworkers, 113; Yorkshire Evening Press, 64, 284; Yorkshire Museum, York, 125, 126, 202, 266; Yorkshire Post, 55, 115, 209, 279; From *With Nature and a Camera*, R. Kearton (Cassell, 1897), 206; Mr W. Hayes, 11, 20, 41, 65, 66, 67, 68, 75, 76, 77, 78, 86, 93, 99, 232, 233, 244, 246, 253, 300; Mr R. H. Hayes, 127, 130, 151, 194; Miss C. D. Sumner, 24, 26, 29, 47, 53, 250, 260, 283, 295; Mr J. Edenbrow, 9, 57, 83, 148, 149; Mrs D. Hague/Mr P. Atkinson, 133, 134, 139, 141, 142, 143; Mr A. E. Witty, 129, 132, 136, 144; Mr B. Arundel, 36, 37, 264, 285; Mr N. Creaser, 137, 138, 145; Mr A. Conner, 10, 146; Mr D. Joy, 234, 235; Mrs M. R. Hartley, 16; Mr D. S. Hall, 33; Mrs J. Hall, 12, 257; Mrs S. Willis, 22; Mr M. Heseltine, 13; Mr T. Bell, 15; Mr W. S. Schofield, 32; Mrs C. Clubley, 84; Mr J. W. Collier, 85; Mrs M. E. Hartley, 111; Mr T. G. Willey, 121; Miss M. Ringrose, 140; Mr J. Scarr, 155; Mrs E. Walker, 158; Mr W. Raw, 161; Mr R. B. Brown, 160; Mrs M. Farnell, 81, 163; Miss J.

Raw, 159; Mrs N. Raw, 164; Miss M. Tunstall, 165, 199; Dr and Mrs J. Farrer, 167; Mrs B. Lyth, 173; Mrs E. Armstrong, 177; Robert Thompson Craftsmen Ltd., 170; Mr L. Rukin, 189; Mr L. Barker, 110; Mr L. E. Malkin, 190; Mr W. Mason, 223; Mrs W. Mason, 191; Mrs J. Massarella, 196; Mr M. Brown, 205; Mr J. Sinclair, 221; Mr T. Hunt, junr., 243; Mr J. Burrows, 198; Mrs W. Guy, 245; Miss H. Holmes, 17, 256; Mr H. Sutcliffe, 290; Mr A. Woodhouse, 296; Mr M. Limbert, 153; Mrs C. A. Kitcher, 87; Mr G. Hare, 299; Mr T. Hunt, 301. Fifty photographs are by Marie Hartley and the rest from the Hartley/Ingilby archives.

I

· *Landscape · People · Homes* ·

A group of photographs depicting the different regions of Yorkshire – vale and coast, dales, hills and moors, industrial landscapes – set the scene and point to the extent and variety of aspects of the county; whilst several photographs of country lanes remind us of the former peace and slow-moving traffic.

Very few photographs are without people in them, shown working, playing or just at home. They are all sorts and conditions of men and women with, where possible, individual stories. They can only be a selection, and there is no attempt to emphasise the great and famous; for that we must refer the reader to our book *Yorkshire Portraits*. Many immigrants had been drawn to the West Riding in the previous century – the Irish, Italians, German merchants to Bradford, German pork butchers to towns, the Jews to Leeds, to mention a few – and integrated into Yorkshire life.

In 1900 the upper classes lived in style, the middle classes in comfort, and the working classes in insecurity. Yet happiness was not the prerogative of any one group. 'A woman's place is in the home', and 'Children should be seen and not heard', or

'Waste not want not
Or you will live to say
Oh how I wish I had that dish
That once I threw away'

were general maxims. Thrift was a dominant Yorkshire characteristic.

At the beginning of the century, churches and Nonconformist chapels were still the centres of community life, binding it together and upholding standards of behaviour through services, Sunday schools and classes. Duty linked with discipline was the ethos of many people. Schools for all had been built, although it was not until 1918 that the half-time system (part work part school) was abolished and the school leaving age raised from twelve to fourteen.

By 1950 secularisation had decimated church and chapel congregations, and rigid class distinctions had partially broken down as people moved up and down the social scale.

Privilege was less obvious, comfort more widespread and prosperity more evenly distributed. Slum clearance started in the early years of the century, gathered pace in the 1930s and continued after 1950, and housing estates with semi-detached villas spread out from cities and towns, often alongside main roads, in what became known as ribbon development. Some villages, such as Linton near Wetherby, were taken over by the large houses of the better-off, and commuting to work became a practice. The houses shown here range from stately homes (nowadays usually open to the public), to terrace housing, suburban villas, farmhouses, cottages, and abandoned homes in the remote parts of the dales, the latter only too poignant reminders of the migration of people from countryside to towns.

BROAD ACRES

1
The broad acres of Yorkshire. The
Vale of York seen from Sutton
Bank. In the far distance are the
hills of the Pennine dales and in the
foreground, Lake Gormire
(1950s).

VALE AND DALE

2
The River Ouse at Cawood, joined by the waters of several Yorkshire rivers – the Ure, the Nidd, and the Wharfe. Cawood was once a market town, an important staging post for traffic on the river with coal staiths, and a venue for salmon fishers up to about 1940. The ferry-crossing was replaced by a swingbridge in 1872. (1938).

3
Lilla Cross near Eller Beck on the old road from Whitby Abbey to Hackness in the midst of the North York Moors.

4
Ingleborough in the Yorkshire Dales (designated as a National Park in 1954) from near Gunnerfleet on Winterscales Beck which flows down Chapel-le-Dale and becomes the River Doe.

COASTAL LANDSCAPES

5
The chalk cliffs of Flamborough
Head between Bridlington and
Filey.

6
Spurn Head, the south-eastern spit
of land on the Yorkshire coast
between the North Sea and the
Humber estuary, seen from the
lighthouse in 1938. At that date, it
was a military post approached the
three and three-quarter miles from
Easington by a light railway which
finished in 1951. It had a school
from 1893 to 1945. Many of the
buildings seen in the photograph
have now gone, and have been
replaced by others.

INDUSTRIAL LANDSCAPES

7
Milnsbridge in the Colne Valley; industrial landscape in 1938 before the Clean Air Act of 1956. John Crowther's mill is in the foreground (the mill dam has now been filled in), and beyond, a train is about to cross the Milnsbridge viaduct on the Huddersfield to Manchester line. On the far left is Nettleton Hill – 'a vast expanse of moor swelling and sinking in sombre majesty to the edge of the horizon' (Phyllis Bentley).

8
Brodsworth Colliery, near Doncaster, then the largest colliery in Yorkshire. Headstocks, chimneys, buildings and new villages invaded the rolling farm lands of South Yorkshire. Brodsworth was opened in 1905 to tap the coveted Barnsley seam, and 5000 to 6000 tons of coal were raised each day (1950s).

9
Halifax from Beacon Hill about 1946, seen through a pall of smoke from mill chimneys and cooling towers illustrating the saying 'Where there's muck, there's money'. The Clean Air Act and the recession of the textile industry have, however, reduced both the muck and the money and smoke has disappeared from the West Riding. Halifax itself has undergone one of the biggest stone-cleaning campaigns in the country, and has preserved its beautiful Piece Hall, a remarkable monument to the textile industry.

COUNTRY LANES

10
A. Conner driving fifty Hereford bullocks from Swaythorpe, Thwing, on the Wolds to Bridlington market (1954).

11
On the way to work in Sleightholme Dale, near Kirkbymoorside (1920s).

12
A quiet lane at
Laughton-en-le-Morthen in South
Yorkshire in the 1890s. The
beautiful church spire, comparable
with that of Patrington, is a
landmark for many miles.

13
Matt Heseltine bringing home the
milk in backcans on panniers on
Neddy in a lane near Redmire,
Wensleydale. Donkeys were used at
Redmire and Castle Bolton for
transporting milk when in summer
the cows were milked on the
pastures (1933).

WEDDING GROUPS

14

Thomas Freeman Firth and Mrs Firth and family on the occasion of their golden wedding in 1904 at Flush House, Heckmondwyke. T.F. Firth (1815-1909) was later knighted. In 1867 he had bought Clifton Mills at Bailiff Bridge for the manufacture of carpets, and ran Firths Carpets.

15

Wedding group at Askrigg in 1904. T.W. Bell and Hilda Armstrong and their families. Tom Bell was a platelayer on the Wensleydale line between Hawes and Aysgarth, and they lived at Cams (railway) Cottages near Askrigg for about twenty years until they moved to Ham Hall crossing, near Northallerton.

16
The wedding of Margaret Annie Minnikin and Edward Parker at Aran Grove House in Sutton on Hull in 1908. Margaret ran away from home and went to live in Hull because she did not like her new step-mother. She took a post as a companion where she met Edward Parker, a rope and twine manufacturer, and after the wedding they went to live in Leeds.

17
Some of the wedding guests and the bridegroom, Charles Fox of Barnsley, at the reception at Wharfedale Grange, Ben Rhydding, Ilkley, the home of the bride, M.E. Fox, daughter of T.B. Fox. As the bridal couple left the station for their honeymoon, fog signals were laid along the line to give them 'a right royal send off' (February, 1894).

FAMILIES

18
Marjorie and Jack Ingilby with
their two daughters, Cecily and
Joan, and Jock, an Aberdeen
terrier, at North Deighton, near
Wetherby. Lieut-Colonel Ingilby
served as a regular soldier in the
Gordon Highlanders and was
wounded in the South African war
(1918).

19
Four generations of the Hartley
family, woollen manufacturers, of
Gillroyd Mills, Morley, and
Beeston Mill, Leeds, at the
Knowle, Morley, built by John in
1889. Joseph, one of the author's
great grandfathers, is seated, John,
grandfather, is on the left, his
eldest son, Joseph, on the right and
his daughter, Doris (c.1900).

WEDDING PROCESSION

20

Returning home after the wedding: Jane Harland of Hutton-le-Hole and Charles Hall of Leeds at Hutton (1906).

EDWARDIAN LADIES

21

Edwardian ladies: Amy and Effie Hinchliffe and Midget, a Yorkshire terrier, outside a thatched, rustic summerhouse typical of the era, at Morley in about 1900. They were the daughters of a manufacturer and were never expected to work.

Staunch Congregationalists and Sunday School teachers, they also played the piano (duets) and excelled at embroidery, crocheting, knitting, tatting and poker work. They never married, and Effie (1883-1973) lived to be ninety.

FAMILIES

22

Robert George Seels and his wife, Faith Iredale Seels, and their children (from left to right) Dulcie Faith, Michael, Robert, Lillian and Louie (on the ground) at Mapleyard Farm, Hooton Pagnell, South Yorkshire, in 1906. Robert and a friend went to Canada with a view to finding a farm and sending for his family, but despite many enquiries, he was never heard of again. Faith, who came of Cumbrian yeoman stock, had come to Hooton Pagnell Hall as a ladies maid and was given the tenancy of the farm. Proving herself a good manager, she eventually owned and ran three farms. Dulcie, on the left, married Charles Hardy, a local farmer's son and during the Second World War, when colliery spoil heaps encroached on their land, they moved to East Ayton, near Scarborough taking the family, stock and implements by train. They disembarked at Seamer station and walked the stock to East Ayton.

23

William and Sarah Brown and their daughter, Hilda May, on the doorstep of their home, 33 The Park, Woodlands, near Doncaster, immediately after they had been visited by King George V and Queen Mary, who inspected the new Woodlands Model village on their Yorkshire tour, 9 July, 1912. William Brown was a coal miner at Brodsworth Colliery. Sarah Brown is holding the portrait of the King and Queen (presented to them as a gift), in such a way that disguised the imminent birth of their second daughter (christened Mary Georgina after the King and Queen). Apparently, the royal party visited the Browns by mistake, and should have been conducted to a neighbour who, having redecorated his house in anticipation, was extremely disappointed, whereas the Browns, who had only just moved in and had the most basic furniture, were very flustered.

24

Three generations of the Schultz family. James Georg Schultz (1851-1911) came to London from Langenburg, near Stuttgart, in the 1870s to avoid military service. He met Christiane Egner who was a governess, from the same German village. They married and moved from London, to Birmingham and then to Yorkshire, where they started pork butcher's shops in Batley, Dewsbury, Liversedge and Cleckheaton. Seeking naturalisation, Christiane changed her name to Schofield and died aged sixty in 1922. Two of the sons joined the British army in the First World War, but nonetheless the windows of their shops were broken.

CHURCH AND CHAPEL

25

Rudston Church and the monolith in the churchyard, remarkable for having been a sacred site for over 3000 years. The monolith is the tallest in Britain, 25½ feet high, and the stone was brought from Caton or Cornelian bay ten miles away.

26

Members of the Young Men's class of Liversedge Parish church, aged seventeen to about twenty-seven. They were led by the Rev E.H. Fernie, a bachelor and a very popular vicar of Liversedge from 1936 to 1950. The class met at 1.30 pm at the vicarage for discussions and talks by outside speakers. The vicar left at 2.20 p.m. to be in church by 2.30 p.m. Many went to the war and several were killed (1938).

27

Providence Place Chapel, a handsome Congregational chapel at Cleckheaton. It was opened on 18 May, 1859, cost £12,500 and was raised in eight years. The frontage has six massive Corinthian columns, and the building extends back over twice the width of the front. The mill and chimney alongside have been demolished.

28
Sunday school teacher and scholars
from Rehoboth Chapel, Morley,
on a trip to Batley Park (c.1912).

29
The sewing ladies in the Sunday
school at Hightown Methodist
Chapel (c.1900). They sewed for
bazaars and sales of work to raise
funds for the chapel.

WEST RIDING
CHILDREN

30
Annie (1902-1982) and Teresa
Firth, farmer's daughters of
Greystone Farm, Drighlington.
Aged thirteen, Annie obtained a
Labour Certificate stating that she
had made 350 attendances at school
for five preceding years, and went
to work as a weaver at various mills
until after she married. She left
when her first child was born.
Teresa was also a weaver (c.1910).

31
Boys from the same background as
the Firth girls wearing the typical
suits and hard collars of the period
(c.1910).

32
John Edward and Willie Smith
Schofield, sons of Lewis and Ann
Schofield of Almondbury near
Huddersfield. They were born at
the Radcliffe Arms, Almondbury.
John went into the wholesale
grocery business and Willie became
a joiner making hand-looms often
for export (1905).

DALES CHILDREN

33
Leonard Hall, William Hall and Ernest Hall, sons of Michael and Isobel Hall of Catrigg Farm, near Hawes. Leonard eventually went to work on the railway and William and Ernest became farmers in Wensleydale. The stack sheet was hung up to form a background for the photograph (1908).

34
Cotterdale children in 1935. The three curly-haired ones are Slingers, the three fair-haired ones in the back row are Ivesons and the dark-haired boy was the gamekeeper's son. John Slinger, a farmer, lived there in 1841 together with seven other farmers and seven coal miners working at Cotterdale Pits. Some women were knitters. Today there is one farm and the rest of the land is farmed from elsewhere.

SCHOOLS

35
Church parade, perhaps at Whitsuntide, of girls from the Towers School, Saltburn, in 1925. This was a private boarding and day school for girls founded by Miss Sarah Macpherson (at first in different premises) in the mid 1870s, and as owner and headmistress she continued until 1909, when the school changed hands. It went on until about 1946. The girls wear white coats or costumes, black stockings and shoes and carry mackintoshes, and are walking in a crocodile.

36
The Quaker school at Ackworth near Pontefract founded in 1779. The school is now co-educational, but formerly the boys occupied the East Wing and the girls the West Wing, and the strip known as the Flags, shown here between the two playgrounds, was neutral territory where relations from both wings, here a brother and sister, could meet, talk and parade up and down (1913).

37
Drill at Carlinghow Boys' School in Batley. Drill and organised games formed part of the school routine (1919).

38
Threshfield School, near
Grassington, Wharfedale, in 1937.
The school was founded in 1674 as
a grammar school but is now a
primary school. The children are
playing one of the many skipping
games.

39
Rugby match between Sedbergh
School and Ampleforth College at
Sedbergh on the school playing
fields, with a background of school
buildings and the Howgill Hills,
on 13 November, 1937. Sedbergh
School was founded in the early
sixteenth century, and is now a
major boys' public school.

SUNDAY SCHOOL TREATS

40
Sunday school scholars from Driffield and the surrounding villages on an outing to Bridlington. A Fowler steam engine driven by H.G. Wood of Great Kendale Farm, Driffield, draws two heavy traction engine trucks and three farm wagons crowded with scholars. The extraordinary procession must have caused a sensation (c.1900).

41
Low Farndale Methodist Chapel anniversary celebrations on 27 August, 1926. Led by a band they process from the chapel after Monday afternoon service.

YOUNG WORKERS

42
Young workers at the Wroe 'factory' at Pontefract making Pontefract cakes in 1905. Small lumps of liquorice dough were stamped by hand with a marker with the traditional device of a bird on a gate. The gate symbolises the old gate of the castle and the bird is the owl adopted from the Savile coat of arms. They were still being made by hand in the 1950s, and a skilled worker could stamp 28,000 in a day.

43
Young people leaving Haggas's mill at Ingrow, near Keighley, at noon on Saturday, 22 August, 1908. A series of factory Acts from the first half of the nineteenth century regulated and improved conditions for the employment of children in textile mills.

CHILDREN AT PLAY

44
West Riding children pose for their photographs. The boy sitting on the gate holds a hoop which propelled along roads or pavements by a stick was a popular pastime (early twentieth century).

45
Idyll in a park in the West Riding (early twentieth century).

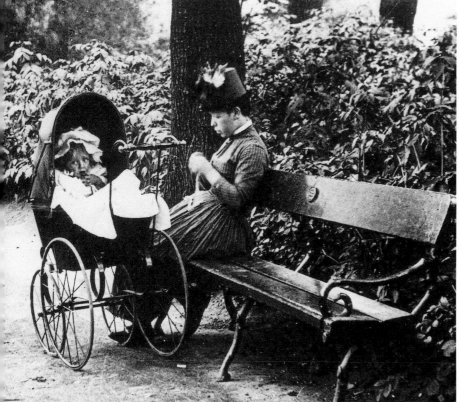

46

Punch and Judy show on the Stray at Harrogate (1938).

47

Donkeys on the sands on the south side at Scarborough in 1913, from a post-card which says on the back 'We are having a lovely time. We have already had two donkey rides. Yesterday we went sailing and were sick'. Note the saddle with pommels to hold on to, and the box for the small child.

FAMILIES AT HOME

48
A coal miner and his child having a meal. This is in Nottinghamshire, but no doubt similar pictures could have been taken in Yorkshire before the days of pithead baths.

49
The Holmes family having dinner in their flat at Quarry Hill, Leeds. William Holmes, aged fifty-six, was unemployed, and his wife, Clara, was fifty-seven. Quarry Hill Flats, designed by the city architect, were completed in 1941 as part of the slum clearance scheme for Leeds. Providing accommodation for 3280 people in 938 flats, they were bold and innovative in concept. But owing to damp and structural defects they were demolished in 1976.

50
Matthew Leadley Winspear and his
wife, Martha, by the fireside of
their home, 6, The Crag, Whitby,
in 1948. Skipper Winspear owned
his own fishing boat 'Progress', and
fished for crabs and lobsters with
his brother out of Whitby. Martha
is knitting a fisherman's guernsey.
Note the well-polished kitchen
range and Tidy Betty and the
valance hung from the mantel
shelf.

51
Muker Show tea, a Yorkshire high
tea consisting of a meat course with
bread and butter, followed by a
variety of pastries, cakes, buns and
biscuits, provided by the Porters of
Gunnerside, Swaledale, for friends
and relatives.

HOMES

52

The great pile of Castle Howard, which Vanbrugh raised for the third Earl of Carlisle from 1701-1714. It was occupied by Queen Margaret's School during the Second World War and during that time the south front and the dome were damaged by fire. It has been restored, and as one of the great houses in Yorkshire is open to the public (1938).

53

Haworth Parsonage in the 1920s, then the residence of the Rev J.C. Hirst, before it became the Brontë Parsonage Museum in 1928. The wing on the right was added after the Brontë's day.

54
Wash day at Queensbury. Well-built terrace houses for mill workers with Black Dyke Mills in the background. The road has pavements but is unmade (1970).

55
Silkstone Row, Altofts, near Wakefield, a remarkable example of terrace housing for coal-miners. The row of fifty-two three-storied houses, smaller terraces behind, a Methodist chapel, a school, a small shop, and a pensioners' club – a complex known as The Buildings – was built by colliery owners, Pope and Briggs, in the 1860s. Needing modernisation, the Row was demolished in the 1970s.

CHANGE

56

Combe House, above Gawthrop, Dent, long abandoned because of its isolated position and falling into ruins. It represents the depopulation of the dales and the emigration to towns. Combe has a beef loft for drying pickled beef for use in winter (1950s).

57

Seacroft Mill near Leeds, one of the many windmills formerly to be found all over the lowlands of Yorkshire as it appeared in the 1950s. It is now part of a hotel complex and is surrounded by houses, multiple stores and other amenities opened in 1965.

II

· *Cities* · *Towns* · *Villages* · *War* ·

The phenomenal rise in the population of industrial towns and cities is often stressed. From a few thousand inhabitants they rose in a century to hundreds of thousands. Sheffield, the largest, had a population of 513,000 in 1951. Leeds was not far behind and with its neighbours, Bradford, Huddersfield, Halifax, Wakefield and all the small towns in between, contained well over a million people in roughly twenty square miles. Industrial towns and cities grew too fast to be well planned, and except for town halls, churches, some chapels and other buildings, were mediocre in appearance and all too alike. In the 1930s, the Headrow in Leeds was driven through tortuous streets and a new civic hall built, and in the 1960s Bradford and Sheffield shed their Victorian images. The Clean Air Act in 1956 started up the sandblasting process so that stonework once more showed a warm brown; slum clearance took time and continued past our period.

Yet loyalty and pride motivated the citizens. We ourselves may have private opinions, but we would not countenance criticism from strangers. Here are the cultural centres: universities, theatres, cinemas, concert halls, libraries, art galleries, museums and also parks. Thinking again of Girtin's Kirkstall Abbey, it is only some thirty or forty miles up the valley of the Aire from Leeds to the limestone country of Malhamdale and other Yorkshire dales.

York is a special case. In 1927 H.V. Morton wrote, 'York is not conscious of its beauty like so many ancient towns; it is too old and too wise and too proud to trick itself out for the admiration of the tourist'. Genteel shabbiness did indeed pervade the streets of York (as it does no longer).

Harrogate and Scarborough, both spas for centuries, might have been described in the early twentieth century as places for the better-off, with the former emphasising treatment for the arthritic and the health-conscious. Again this has all changed. The three photographs of Scarborough taken by one of the old photographers, William Hayes, in the summer season, epitomise the Edwardian era. Seaside resorts filled dual roles – holidays and the fishing industry – and Whitby and the neighbouring fishing villages attracted artists before realism gave way to abstraction, colour photography arrived and picturesque corners were irrevocably changed.

We can only show a few photographs depicting the wealth of the market towns and villages of Yorkshire, usually taken on market or fair days to lend them extra interest. On other days they were quiet until motor transport invaded them. Here, in towns such as Northallerton, Bedale, Stokesley, Yarm and above all Richmond, some idea of the elegance and dignity of the Georgian town lingers.

Finally we include a few photographs of the wars which blighted the first half of the twentieth century. In 1914 the Great War broke out and was followed, as we look back incredulously, by another, so that they came to be called the First and the Second World Wars. As a result of their work in the Great War, women were given the vote (but many lost possible husbands slain on the battlefields). The wars marked important social change, but at what a price!

CITIES

58

Briggate, Leeds, the ancient main
street of Leeds with yards leading
off and also the more recent arcades
– Thornton's and County. There
was a cab rank in the centre, often
sandwich board men slowly trailed
along and bunches of violets and
mimosa were sold in the spring. On
the left were Croisdale's sports
goods and Walker's bookshop, and
on the right Home and Colonial
stores and Walker and Hall's
showroom. Marks and Spencer
now occupies one side (1917).

59

Leeds Town Hall and municipal
offices, library and art gallery on
the right, before they were cleaned
and the art gallery altered. The
town hall built in 1853-8, architect
Cuthbert Broderick, stands at the
bottom of the new Headrow and
symbolises Victorian confidence.

60

Statue in bronze of Richard Oastler with factory children, formerly in Forster Square and now in Rawson Square, Bradford, erected in 1869. Oastler campaigned against the employment of children and for the Ten Hours Bill. Bradford honours some of its great men with public statues: W.E. Forster, M.P. who promoted the national education system in 1870, Sir Titus Salt and Lord Masham in Lister Park, as well as Peel statue in Peel Park (1938).

61

Forster Square, Bradford, decorated for the silver jubilee celebrations of the reign of King George V and Queen Mary in 1935. Different forms of transport fill the streets. The railway station is on the right, soot-blackened buildings hem in the square, and the statue of W.E. Forster stands in the centre.

62

High Street, Sheffield, in the early
twentieth century. On the left was
the entrance to a covered market,
and on the right, Marples Hotel,
hit by a bomb on 12 December,
1940. In two air raids on Sheffield
that month 700 people were killed.
Walsh's drapers is next to it. Other
well-known shops were Cole Bros.
and Cockaynes all now taken over.
This scene is totally changed.

63

The market-place at Hull at the
turn of the century.
Kingston-upon-Hull has been a
port since the fourteenth century,
and its docks and streets with
ancient buildings, make it unique
in Yorkshire. The interior of Hull
Holy Trinity church reminds us of
pictures painted by the Dutch
painter, Saenredam. A statue of
William III by Scheemaker,
erected in 1734, adorns the centre
of the market-place.

YORK

64
St Sampson's Square Market, York, before it was moved to a new site in the 1950s.

65
Monk Bar, York, in the early twentieth century. A hansom cab goes under the arch.

66
A corner of St Sampson's Square market in the early years of the twentieth century.

67
Minster Gates decorated with
bunting for a royal visit in 1900.
The shop on the right is a
fruiterer's adjoined by Loadman,
an antique dealer.

68
The Shambles, York, in its old
guise with open-fronted butchers'
shops (c. 1900).

69

The Stray at Harrogate at the turn
of the century. In the foreground,
wagonettes are filling up with
passengers, and landaus wait on
Prospect Hill. A walled garden,
cleared in 1921, occupies the site of
the War Memorial.

70

The Royal Pump Room,
Harrogate, built in 1842 (c.1900).
From 7 a.m. to 9 a.m. people came
to take the strong sulphur water,
and the roads were cordoned off so
that the drinkers could promenade
and walk to the Crescent Gardens
where a small orchestra played. In
1926, 1500 glasses of water a day
were dispensed. The annexe has
gone and is replaced by a glass
building.

HARROGATE

71

The Turkish Bath cooling room in the Royal Baths at Harrogate. The Royal Baths were built in 1897 at a cost of £120,000, and in about 1900, over thirty different bathing treatments were offered. 'The Turkish Bath,' it was said 'in spite of all rivals, remains the Prince of Baths.' It is still available.

72

The staff of the Royal Baths on the steps leading from Parliament Street to the Winter gardens (c.1900). With so many different bathing treatments, a large staff was necessary to provide individual attention for each client. The recommended length of time for spa treatments was at least three weeks.

MIDDLESBROUGH

73

In the first half of this century,
Middlesbrough was a byword for
dreariness. It had been a boom
town with a population of forty in
1830, rising to 147,000 in 1951.
Industries, based on Durham coal
and ironstone discovered in the
Cleveland Hills, started huge
works producing iron and then
steel, subject to recessions which
punctuate the story of the town. But
the terraces of houses in the
foreground and middle distance
have gone, and a new centre and
new stores have eclipsed the old
Middlesbrough (c.1950).

74

Middlesbrough has two bridges
over the Tees – the famous
Transporter Bridge built in 1911
and farther upstream, Newport
Bridge, opened after twelve years
of debate and conferences on the
crossing in 1934, by which time
unemployment was rife. It was then
described as the first vertical lift
bridge in Britain and the largest of
its kind in the world. It was built
by Dorman Long and Co. who
tendered £436,913, and is here
shown in the lifted position 120 feet
above high water. The tiny figures
on the bridge indicate its size.

SCARBOROUGH

75

The Spa at Scarborough at the turn of the century. The bandstand with almost Moorish architecture was erected in 1858, and replaced in 1912 by the present Sun Enclosure. The band playing may be that of Charles Godfrey junior or a military band.

76

Sunday parade at Scarborough on the Esplanade at the turn of the century. Parasols protect delicate complexions from the sun. The Crown Hotel is on the left and the domes of the Grand Hotel, 'a High Victorian gesture of assertion and confidence' (Pevsner), glimpsed on the right.

77

On the sands at the south side, Scarborough, at the turn of the century. A crowd watches a pierrot troupe, perhaps Catlins, and in the background are several bathing machines, one in the sea, a barrel organ and a booth selling 'Neapolitain Ices'. On the top of Castle Hill, on the left, is the Warwick Revolving Tower, a viewing point. Erected in 1898, it was removed as an eyesore nine years later.

78

The North Bay, Scarborough, in the early twentieth century. 'Something was being prepared far away behind the curtaining of the grey foam, the black rolling waves, something sudden and disastrous . . .' (Osbert Sitwell in *Before the Bombardment*). German warships shelled the town on 16 December 1914.

SEASIDE RESORTS

79

Up to 1861, Saltburn was a small, secluded hamlet noted for smuggling, but when the Stockton to Darlington railway was extended there, a new town emerged becoming a fashionable seaside resort, with a huge hotel, the Zetland, a pier (which is still there), ornamental gardens, a church and chapels. Here, Saltburn-by-the-Sea is seen in its heyday, about 1905.

80

Children's Corner, Filey, with a pierrot troupe entertaining a crowd, and bathing machines on the sands (c. 1900).

81
Bridlington harbour in 1920. The
two main industries of the coast –
fishing and tourism – join forces
when local fishermen take visitors
for trips on the sea in their cobles.

82
The beach at Hornsea, one of the
smaller seaside resorts of the
Yorkshire coast, in about 1911.
Bathing tents were then all the rage,
giving the beach the appearance of a
medieval military encampment.

MARKET TOWNS

83
Tin Ghaut, Whitby, with Fair Isle Cottage approached through a wicket, in about 1946. Many writers and artists found inspiration at Whitby, in its history, its red roofs and its picturesque corners, of which Tin Ghaut was one. Its site is now a car park.

84
The market-place at Driffield in the East Riding. The Bell Hotel, on the left, was then the centre throughout the year for buying grain, and the hotel conveyance, which met customers at the station, waits in front. The fountain just glimpsed in the middle of the photograph has gone. Agricultural implements, fruit, potatoes and other goods are displayed for sale (early twentieth century).

85

Helmsley market-place early in this century. The monument in Gothic style, sheltering a statue of the second Lord Feversham, was erected in 1869, and it quite overshadows the restored medieval cross seen below the church tower. How elegant and unobtrusive are the carts and traps compared with motor cars.

86

The market-place at Pickering in the 1920s. The town, once in the forest of Pickering with a castle dating from the twelfth century, has had a market since at least 1201. It serves the people of the moorlands and the Vale of Pickering.

87

A performing bear in front of the Shambles in the market-place at Settle. The two children on the left are the grandchildren of the photographer, E.R. Wethey of Redcar, on holiday at Clapham. The shops include Brown, tailor, draper, clothier, hatter and bootmaker; S. Hodgson, cabinet-maker and upholsterer; Rowlandson, tinner and brazier; Walthery, hairdresser; and Hunt's cycle repairing depot (1903).

88

Richmond market-place in 1906. The shop of George King and sons, saddlers, abuts on to the tower of Holy Trinity church. Charles Todd, hairdresser and tobacconist, is to the right of Kings. Beyond, James Beagarie displays his baskets next to Fawcett, milliner. Past the cross is the Bishop Blaize Hotel and Blade's hair cutting rooms. Boots and shoes are displayed in the foreground, and a woman with luggage waits by a carrier's covered wagon. The shops round the church were demolished in the 1920s.

89

Fair day at Skipton-in-Craven in the early twentieth century. In spring and November fairs for horned cattle were held in the High Street, before auction marts took over the trade.

90

Yarm October Fair in 1938. 'The fair was formerly one of the largest in the north of England, between 300 and 400 wagons and carts laden with cheese arriving in the town' (Bulmer, 1890).

Askrigg

VILLAGES

91

West Burton in Wensleydale, a village with an extensive green, where fairs were formerly held for horses, cattle and sheep on 10 March and 6 May. It had a customary market, and the obelisk is dated 1820 (1904).

92

Askrigg in Wensleydale, seen in the early years of this century, a street village and formerly a market-town. The Old Hall on the left (built in 1678) was burnt down in 1935. The adjoining Manor House and Kings Arms Hotel were built by John Pratt, racehorse owner, as his home in 1767.

93

Coxwold in the Howardian Hills, the quintessential picturesque village with many old houses, including Shandy Hall where Laurence Sterne, vicar of Coxwold, lived from 1760-68. The church standing high above the street completes the scene. The large wych elm has gone (c.1910).

94

Stainland near Elland, a typical hill top village in the West Riding. It has a church, chapel, Mechanics Institute, and a village school, seen to the right (1938).

95
Lockton on the edge of the North York Moors in 1938. Smoke rising from the chimneys fills the air with the scent of burning peat.

96
Robin Hood's Bay seen from Brickhills at the top of the Bank in the early nineteenth century. It looks much the same today except that the large shed, once a cart-shed adjoining the stables for the horses used locally, and two houses on the cliff edge, have gone. The drying ground was allocated to householders paying 1s. a year, and clothes or sheets were sometimes used to signal messages to husbands passing by on ships (1910).

97
Pond at the Wold village of Fridaythorpe (1938). Many ponds have been drained and have gone without trace. They were used for watering stock and after work the horses were walked round in the water to wash their legs.

98
Newton-upon-Rawcliffe near Pickering in the 1930s. The village then had two large ponds and this one has now gone. The other can just be glimpsed farther up the green.

Members of the Women's Land Army harvesting on a farm near Kirkbymoorside in 1917. The Land Army was formed in that year, and by July 1918 there were 113,000 members, some working on the land, some in forestry or forage. They were told to 'dress like a man, but to behave like a British girl who expects chivalry and respect from all' (A. Marwick).

100

The munitions factory at Barnbow, near Leeds, where many women were employed during the First World War. The work was hard and dangerous; on 5 December 1916, a shell exploded in one of the fusing rooms just as the night shift was starting operations killing thirty-five people. The other workers carried on their work without interruption. A second explosion, killing two girls, occurred on 21 March, 1917, and another on 31 May, 1918, killed three men.

101

H.R.H. The Princess Royal escorted by Major J.F. Fearon, inspects Green Howards recruits and reservists of No. 2 Infantry Company at the Depot, Richmond, in April 1940.

102

Doncaster market-place in 1917. The mayor and civic party stand on top of a tank, recently returned from the western front, bearing the name 'Egbert'. They are launching a war savings appeal to pay for battle tanks. The poster at the top, calling the Germans 'huns' was typical of the hatred expressed at that time.

WORLD WAR II

103
A Handley-Page Halifax Mark 3 aircraft being loaded with incendiary bombs ready for an attack on the enemy 'somewhere in Yorkshire' in late 1944 or early 1945. None of these aircraft, of which more than 6000 were built, have survived to the present day.

104
A Victory Street Party in Park Street off Moorfield Road, Armley, Leeds (1945).

III

· Industries · Fishing · Farming ·

The great industries of Yorkshire – coal, textiles, iron and steel – are epic stories of man's exploitation of the resources at hand, of the inventiveness and vision of the pioneers and of the skills of the work force. Nowadays we look at the huge mills with awe, conscious of the men who, starting from modest beginnings but living in auspicious times, conceived and built them. Our period is the last phase of the Yorkshire textile industry, subject to slumps, but then pre-eminent in its field as producer and exporter of cloth, with Bradford as the acknowledged world centre for the sale of wool. In the 1950s there were over 1000 firms and over 200,000 operatives, or in other words, mills and soaring chimneys belching smoke filled the valleys of the West Riding, and workers summoned by buzzers flocked to the factories. Although wages were never large, strikes were rare.

The coal industry is a different story, basic to other industries but itself fraught with danger and strife. In the first half of the century, the Yorkshire coalfield was the largest and the most productive in the country. Like the textile industry it was an integral part of daily life in the West Riding, with colliers seen going home in their 'pit dirt' and pits closing in the north of the field and others opening farther south. Tragic accidents have punctuated its story as well as tragic strikes and that of 1926 has gone down to posterity. In our period, new modern pits were opened, new techniques were introduced, and – imperative for welfare – pit-head baths were built in the late 1930s. When in 1947 the mines were nationalised, hopes ran high.

Sheffield, too, has a proud history, in both the making of fine cutlery and silverware and the enormous presses forging huge components in cavernous workshops, like scenes from Wagner's *Ring*. Sheffield can boast a gallery of famous sons and famous firms internationally known. Elsewhere, there were other companies in the West Riding where railway, steam and mill engines were made. A recent letter to us from an engineer machinist who served his time from

1919 to 1924 recalls, 'The loyalty of the work force cannot be imagined.' The industries of Yorkshire were and are legion.

Fishing on the coast and agriculture on its broad acres are industries anciently pursued and foremost in the story of Yorkshire. In our era, the days of sailing craft and dramatic scenes of them battling to regain harbours in storms and lifeboats setting out on perilous rescues had gone, although the latter is still a dangerous operation. Cobles, the traditional craft, remain, but fishing has diminished in the coastal villages. Hull, Scarborough, Whitby and Bridlington are the fishing ports. At Hull in the 1940s a hundred or more trawlers sailed and landed 1000 tons of fish daily. Whitby, with keel boats and cobles, was of less importance than Scarborough, where better quality fish was landed. But in September, both were visited by the Scottish fisher girls and the herring fleets sailing down the coast from Lerwick to Lowestoft. Barrels of salt herrings were exported to Germany, Russia and Poland, a trade diminishing in the 1930s and ceasing in the '50s.

Farming may be classified into two groups – arable and pastoral – and the emphasis is on the large work force with time to express pride in work. A fine series of photographs has come from the Wolds, many of them located for us by Mr W.W. Gatenby of Rudston. A typical Wolds farm had 400 to 500 acres, but a few were bigger, and all were notable for the large staff employed and the hierarchy of jobs. Horses, pulling Wold wagons and all the implements, required many horsemen. But as the 1940s drew to a close, tractors and combine harvesters were soon to revolutionise the system, so that horses on the farm and threshing days have almost vanished and the cost of sophisticated equipment is astronomical. Similarly, in the pastoral dales in about 1950, tractors replaced horses to drive hay-making and other machinery. The old days have gone, but they may occasionally be looked back on with nostalgia.

GREAT MILLS

105

Salt's mill and the model village of
Saltaire, near Shipley, built
between 1850 and 1871 by Sir
Titus Salt who commented that
'. . . the task of improving the
conditions of the working-classes,
however difficult and laborious it
may be, is not thankless or
unprofitable.' Salt's closed as a
textile mill in 1986.

106

Manningham Mills, Bradford,
built in 1873 by Samuel Cunliffe
Lister, later raised to the peerage.
The frontage of the mill stretches
one third of a mile. This and other
great mills, Dean Clough at
Halifax and Black Dyke at
Queensbury, epitomise the heyday
of the Yorkshire textile industry.

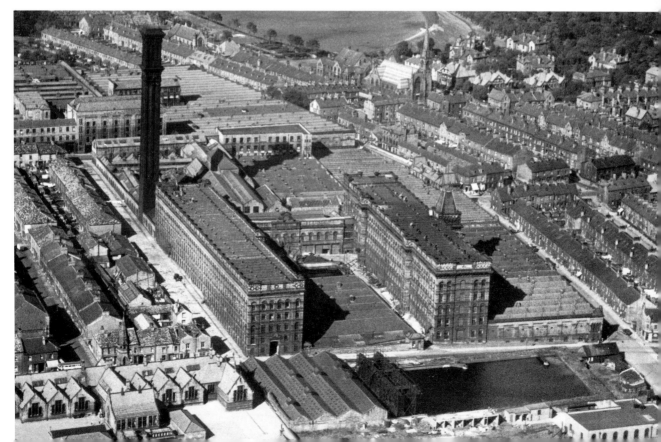

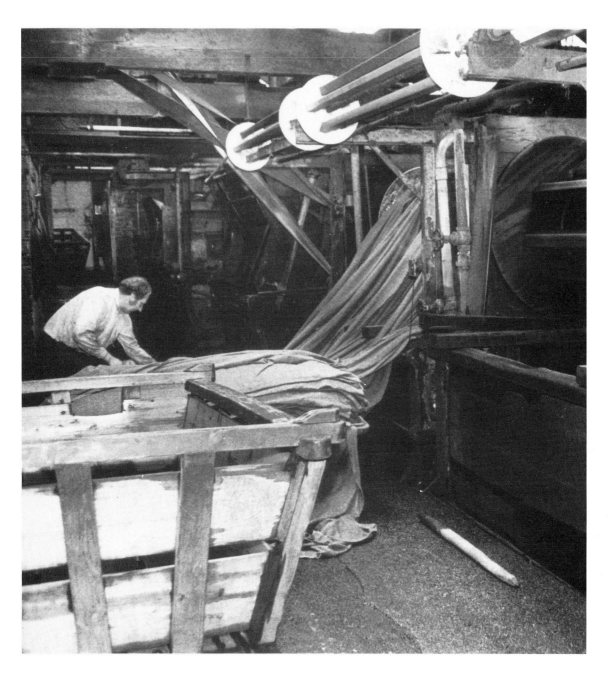

WOOL AND CLOTH

107
A team of four warehousemen, two filling and two treading, packing wool into a sheet at William Fison's, Greenholme Mill, Burley. The sheet was slung on two cords, and when filled, the open sides were pulled together with a *jerry* (double hooks) and skewered (c.1907).

108
R. Zolts working in the dyehouse of the Crank Mill, Morley. The mill, built in 1790 for £1,250 by Lord Dartmouth and leased out, was the first steam-powered woollen mill in Yorkshire.

MILL ENGINE

109

No. 2 mill engine at the Slaithwaite
Spinning Company's mill. It was a
tandem compound horizontal
engine, about 1000 h.p., called
'Fearless' and was installed in 1883
by Pollitt and Wigzell. Dismantled
by J. Sykes and Son, boiler and
machinery merchants, Slaithwaite,
in 1923.

LOOMS

110
The boiler house at Nutclough Mill, Hebden Bridge. (The mill was built in 1870 as a co-operative venture.) The boilers fired the steam engine above them, which powered the machinery of the mill. Here they have been modernised by the installation of hoppers for feeding with coal or coke. Formerly it was shovelled by a brawny, sweating firer straight into the red-hot fire (c.1916).

111
The weaving shed at W.E. Crowther's Crimble Mill at Slaithwaite in the Colne Valley in 1938. It held about sixty Dobcross looms weaving reasonably priced tweeds, the staple trade of the valley. The mill closed in 1976.

COAL MINERS

112
The under manager and four miners in a stall at the coal face in Maltby Main Colliery. Maltby was a modern colliery opened in 1911, and pithead baths were built in 1938, the date of this photograph. Over a million tons of coal were produced in a year.

113
Coal miners having their *snap* (meal) underground. An early photograph, whereabouts unknown (c. 1900).

114
Coal miners manning a soup
kitchen at Darfield, near Barnsley,
during the General Strike in 1926.
When the miners struck against
lower wages and longer hours they
were locked out (1 May).
Thousands of other workers came
out in sympathy for nine days, but
the miners suffering hardship held
out until November.

115
Underground workers at
Dodsworth Colliery, near
Barnsley, rehearsing for a carol
service with the Dodsworth Miners
Welfare Band at the pit bottom
(December, 1961).

SHEFFIELD

116
Fifteen-ton steam-powered drop hammer, weighing over 200 tons, at the Vickers Works in Sheffield in the Second World War. For the first eighteen months of the war, this was the only hammer forging crankshafts for Spitfire engines, manned by two teams of eight men each shift. It was so precious that it was guarded night and day.

117
Buffer girls in one of the Sheffield Spoon and Fork Buffing shops where time and motion studies were carried out in 1920. The buffer girls (polishers) of Sheffield were notoriously wild. The red head scarf, worn when they came out of the works, identified them, together with black or hessian aprons – never a coat or shawl was worn. There were many small cutlery workshops besides the well-known firms of Mappin and Webb and Walker and Hall.

MINE AND FORGE

118

Two ironstone miners in Lumpsey
Mine, inland from Skinningrove,
Cleveland. The mine was sunk in
1881 and closed in 1954. Sites of
eighty-three ironstone mines have
been listed in Cleveland stretching
from Rosedale in the south, in
Eskdale, along the coast from
Whitby to Saltburn and inland to
Guisborough and Great Ayton
(c.1900-1910).

119

Tending a furnace at Kirkstall
Forge on the River Aire near Leeds
in about 1950. The forge has a long
history and was run by the Butler
family from 1779. Its products
have been, and still are, legion,
ranging from spades to back axles.

FISHERWOMEN

120

Fisherwomen at Staithes evidently selling fish to a dealer. The women, no less than the men, had a hard life collecting bait, getting soaked to the skin, baiting the nets and suffering the loss of their menfolk in storms. The artist, Laura Knight, who lived at Staithes for fourteen years noted that the toil was great and the recompense small (c. 1900).

121

Scottish fisher girls, working for Scottish curers at Scarborough in the 1930s. 'Gipping' (cleaning and gutting) herrings which were roughly salted in the 'farlins' (large wooden troughs). 'One girl could gut sixty to seventy herrings a minute . . . 20,000 in a day.' (Bochel).

WHITBY SCENES

122
Jack Wale, Jack Hebden and
George Leadley (looking on)
making crab pots on the quay at
Whitby (1938).

123
Dutch fishermen drying their nets
at Whitby (1950s). The ports of the
Yorkshire coast have age-old
connections with the Netherlands.

FISH CATCH AND EGG COLLECTING

124

Dick Cross leading the donkey, Boy Brown, on the right and George (Aaron) Major in the trilby engaged in winter fishing for cod and haddock at North Landing, Flamborough, in 1938. Seventy years ago, there were sixty to eighty cobles under sail here and the fish were washed and gutted in big tubs, then packed into boxes at the top of the cliff and sent off by rail to Manchester and other towns. All the fishermen kept donkeys, and the cobles themselves were built at Flamborough. Fishing here became uneconomic, and in 1986 only two cobles went out crabbing in summer.

125

Collecting eggs at Bempton on the Yorkshire coast in the early years of the century. Harry Marr is descending the cliff and three Hodgsons are holding him. There were several gangs of 'climmers', some were fishermen and some farm labourers, who collected eggs between Bempton and Flamborough from the middle of May until the end of June. In a good season, thousands of eggs, mainly guillemots, were gathered. Special coloured eggs were collectors' pieces, but the bulk were despatched to Manchester, Leeds and other places for food. In 1954, an Act of Parliament stopped the practice.

126

Harry Marr of Buckton and the tackle of a 'climmer'. Round his shoulder is a scoop for reaching for eggs. Usually a 'climmer' wore a harness and at one time a policeman's helmet.

ARABLE FARMING

127
Edgar Dowson and his team plough a first furrow near Hutton-le-Hole in 1947.

128
Harrowing in the Vale of Pickering in the 1930s.

129
Drilling roots at Fimber Field on
the Wolds with a Russell's of
Kirkbymoorside drill. This had a
glass bottom which enabled fine
fertiliser to be dropped
simultaneously down the drill on
either side of the seed. Note the
men's bell-bottomed trousers.

130
John Wass harvesting oats in West
Gill, Farndale, with Jim Lumsdon
leading the horses (1938).

THRESHING

131
The Thackrays of Brawby in the Vale of Pickering starting out with their threshing set. John Thackray, with the white beard, and his three sons, Jack with the child in his arms, Frank with the little girl and James by the big wheel (c.1900).

132
The Ireland's remarkable stackyard at Pilmoor near Brafferton in the Vale of York during the First World War. Matt Ireland holds the horse harnessed to a cart filled with mangolds and J.W. Ireland stands on the right. These boat-shaped stacks required great skill to build. Each took two days to thatch and contained a full day's threshing. Just one in a stackyard was dubbed an 'achievement stack'.

WOLD WAGONS

133

A Wold wagon drawn by four horses laden with sacks of grain at Sunderland Wick, Driffield. The wagoner carrying sacks of grain skilfully dropped them on to the wagon in exactly the right place to build up his load (early 1920s).

134

A rulley laden with wool sheets at a farm near Driffield about to set off for the railway station. What skill and pride in work the pyramid represents!

FARM STAFF

135
The plough boy C.R.Dykes, aged sixteen, harrowing wheat with his team of horses – Farmer, Daisy and Depper – at Thornthorpe near Langton, on the Wolds, in October 1910. His wage, plus keep and lodging, was £15 for the year, rising to £20 in 1913. He took great pride in his horses which were 'groomed up like racehorses'.

136
The staff at High Mowthorpe, one of the largest farms on the Wolds, 1000 acres, in 1911 when the farmer was Charles Nessfield (not in the photograph). On the left back row is Amos Witty, foreman, next to him Haigh, gamekeeper. The group also includes Greenlagh, shepherd, Herbert Burks, foreman's lad, and wagoner, wagoner's lad, third lad (thoddy), fourth lad (fouerdy), Alf Witty and three Witty children. Note the corduroy waistcoats with calicoe sleeves which were comfortable regular wear.

THRESHING DAY

137
Threshing day at John Burdass's farm, Dotterill Park, Kilham, on the Wolds. This is a large farm of 636 acres. Three wagons wait ready to transport the grain (1912).

138
The team for the threshing day at Dotterill Park, Kilham. The tall man in the centre is Newsome Walker, the engine man (1912).

PLOUGHING

139

A ploughing day on a farm on the
Wolds. When a new man took over
a farm it was customary for his
neighbours to give him a ploughing
day because he needed help to finish
his ploughing. Here there are
seven ploughs and teams in action;
but even a small farmer would
probably be given five.

140

A ploughing match at Ainderby
Quernhow in the Vale of York. H.
Lightfoot junior from Kirby
Grindalythe is ploughing (1940s).

HORSES

141
Wagons and horses at Fimber Field near Sledmere engaged in the annual driving competition organised on the Sledmere estate by Sir Mark Sykes who, prior to the First World War, realised the potential for field-battery driving and formed the Wagoners Reserve. In 1914, 200 drivers put their horses and green-painted wagons through exacting routines competing for various prizes. They were called up and their officers were termed 'Road Masters'. The Wagoners Memorial in the village commemorates their war service (1912).

142
Stallion parade at the Yorkshire Shire Horse Show held at Cross Hill, Driffield (1920s).

143
Seven wagons, each drawn by four horses, carrying corn from Cowlam, then one of the largest farms on the Wolds – 2000 acres (c.1912). In 1928, Cowlam was divided into four farms.

144
A horse, held by the wagoner, decorated for a show with real white daisies (later artifical flowers were used), at Fimber Field, near Sledmere (1920s).

SHEEP AND PIGS

145
A once typical scene on the Wolds –
sheep folded on turnips on Dotterill
Park Farm, Kilham (c.1912). A
new fold was made every day, and
some turnips were lifted and
chopped in the turnip cutter, and
others left to be eaten in the rows.

146
Large White pigs in a Wolds dale
on Park Farm, Langtoft, farmed
by M. Conner who then kept a
small herd of Large Whites
(1950).

PEAS AND POTATOES

147
Pea pickers in the Selby district.
They were recruited by the farmer
and transported by lorry to the
field. Having filled a sack, the
picker took it to be weighed and
was paid at so much a sack (1938).
In the early years of the century the
pay was 1d. a peck and a bag held 5
pecks. Children picked during the
holidays.

148
Planting potatoes at Leathley near
Otley in 1943.

149
Liquorice plants growing at
Pontefract (1940s). The liquorice
gardens of Pontefract, where the
soil is deep and sandy, inspired the
making of liquorice sweets,
especially Pontefract cakes, in that
region. Liquorice has many
medicinal properties, as extolled by
Gerard. In West Riding towns, the
roots sold at greengrocers were
chewn for their sweet juice, and
small pieces of black stick liquorice
from chemists, shaken up in water
in a bottle, made a favourite
childish drink called Spanish water.

150
Richard Smith and George Rhodes
harvesting rhubarb at Thorpe Lane
Farm, near Wakefield. Because of
several favourable conditions –
climate, coal for heating the forcing
sheds – 95% of the rhubarb grown
in Europe was produced in the
country between Leeds and
Wakefield.

TURF AND PEAT

151
George Breckon of Duck House, Farndale, North York Moors, leading turf on a sledge on Blakey Moor to make a turf stack for winter fuel (1938).

152
J. Atkinson leading peats with a coup cart to West End, Lunds, upper Wensleydale. Some peats are drying on the ground and others have been built into conical stacks (1936).

153
Besides peat being cut for centuries on the high moorlands of the North Riding, it has also been an ancient source of fuel in the low lying land of the Thorne/Hatfield area near the River Don in South Yorkshire. In the 1880s, peat took on a new significance as animal litter and at Thorne, several companies established manufacturing mills on the edge of the peat moorland. Here, a load of peat is being taken in a horsedrawn wagon along one of the Thorne Moor's tramways to Moorends Mill to be processed and packed ready for despatch by rail (c.1896).

SWALEDALE SHEEP

154

The Sheep Farmer. William Pratt (1883-1950) of High Houses, Snaizeholme, off upper Wensleydale, seeing to his sheep at the time of a freak snowstorm in May, 1935. There were then nine small farms occupied in Snaizeholme. (Now most of the houses are used as second homes and the land is farmed from away.)

155

James Scarr and helper with Swaledale tups at Coleby Hall, near Bainbridge, in 1912. The formation of the Swaledale Sheep Breeders Association in 1919 stressed new points for breeding, for instance, a white nose instead of a motley face, and the removal of 'kemps' (hairs) from the back.

SHEEP CLIPPING

156
Leonard and James Scarr and
helpers of Coleby Hall, upper
Wensleydale, clipping sheep in
Sargill Park, on Abbotside. Here,
in the Middle Ages, the abbot and
monks of Jervaulx Abbey
depastured their cattle (1930s).

SHEEP WASHING

157

Sheep washing at Cow Dub, Dent, in about 1910, with the Dent Head viaduct of the Settle-Carlisle line in the background. Two men, probably wrapped in fleeces, as was the practice, stand in the river, and 3000 sheep were washed in one day.

158

The crowd of farmers and their families at Stean sheep washing, upper Nidderdale, in 1906. These events, when washing preceded clipping, were then social occasions. Sheep washing is discontinued but because of depopulation, it is unlikely that such numbers of local people would be there today.

HAYMAKING

159
Haymaking at Muker, Swaledale. Christopher Raw is raking and Thomas William Raw, John Hunter and an Irishman sharpen their long-handled scythes. Note the strickle attached to the scythe of John Hunter for balance (1920s).

160
The end of haytime near Low Row, Swaledale (1920s). Two of the men hold knag rakes used for the last raking up of the meadows, and the man on the left holds what appears to be a small hand sweep.

OTHER JOBS

161

Frank Clapham with a flock of geese in Hawes Cattle Market. He was a carrier and smallholder at Askrigg and had a wagonette for driving visitors out on excursions. He bought geese in August/September and shod them in tar and sand in troughs in the garth at the west end of Penny Garth, Hawes. Driving them at about twelve miles a day, he then sold them to farmers in the Bedale-Northallerton area to feed on the stubble (1910-20).

162

Muck spreading near Park House, upper Swaledale, in the 1950s. Manure from the field barns was taken on to the fields by horse and coup cart and raked out at intervals in small heaps, which were then spread evenly by hand with forks. Sometimes the latter job was let out at the rate of ½d. or 1d. a heap.

COWS

163
Cow-shed on G. Parker's Tunnerford Farm, Keasden, near Clapham. Above the cow's head can be seen a witch-stone (a stone with a hole through it) hanging from a beam. It has been there many years to protect the cows.

164
Amelia and Nellie Alderson milking Shorthorn cows out on the pasture on an upland farm, Stone House, upper Swaledale (1928).

IV

· *Occupations* · *Shops* ·

The majority of occupations illustrated are the self-employed, the unusual or the rare, and by and large, the captions are self-explanatory. Beginning with the professions, we see the vicar and his verger, the doctor, the botanist, the writer and the sculptor. It is appropriate that we salute the old photographers who left valuable and delightful records of past life. J.B. Priestley, whose *Good Companions* was published in 1929, is one of the distinguished band of Yorkshire authors who flourished then and later. What first-rate novels, with good stories and well-drawn characters, we read in those days (not only by Yorkshire writers), brought to our notice by the long reviews in literary magazines.

Craftsmen – shoemakers, blacksmiths, joiners – oiled the wheels of daily life, and in towns the cabinet-makers, tailors, saddlers, coopers and tinners supplied individual wants, supplemented in the West Riding by the potteries that made both domestic and ornamental goods. Very few photographs depict women's work in the home. The fireplace with kettles,

pictured at the Wagon and Horses, Saltersgate, points only too well to the former primitive cooking and washing arrangements. All the same home baking was the rule. Electricity, arriving in the 1920s, brought with it labour saving devices; sanitation became more general, and the production of nylon in 1937, followed by other synthetic fibres, eventually revolutionised clothing and much besides. The throwaway society was born.

Many more people than one imagines were on the move in streets and on roads, walking or with a horse and a conveyance. Walking was a necessity, not relegated as it is nowadays to a hobby. The carrier with his covered cart has had inadequate recognition, providing as he did a network for the transport of essential goods before both railways and motor services. Hawkers called their wares and tailors, shoemakers, Scotch drapers, umbrella menders, knife grinders and others travelled on their rounds whilst a rare circus or menagerie, a foreigner with a performing bear, or an organ grinder with monkey brought entertainment.

Elephants have been seen in the streets of Hawes, and we ourselves remember the square at Wetherby filled with Wombwell's Menagerie in the 1920s.

Shops, on the whole, belong to towns, but corner and village shops had much in common. For a variety of reasons, they have declined in numbers. At Askrigg nine (now two) are remembered, some consisting only of cottages 'selling out of the living room', and similarly there were a dozen in Dent Town. One of the shops at Askrigg, a chemist's, was the first in the dale to sell rouge, and people came from afar in traps to buy it. In market towns, a traditional combination was the grocer and draper. The former bought in butter and cheese, and sold goods in return.

Formerly, as is well known, many shops in towns were privately owned and individualistic. There were chain stores, such as the Maypole, which had damp sawdust on the floor and mounds of butter on the counters so that sales were accompanied by the sounds of butter hands slapping it into pounds. Grocers' shops were to be found in town centres as they are not today. Hams for sale hung from the ceilings, and goods were sold loose, packed and dexterously folded in paper bags. The fragrant aroma of coffee roasting permeated the air of the streets outside some cafés and grocers. Chemists featured tall carboys of coloured liquid in their windows and wrapped goods in thick white paper, sealed with red sealing wax.

Ironmongers sold tinned goods rather than plastic. Fish shops had water running down the windows to keep the fish cool, and butchers, poulterers and green-

grocers arranged massed displays for Christmas. At this time, the market halls of cities and large towns were marvels of plenty, with goods sold fresh without deep freezing. Drapers had underclothes in boxes and displayed ribbons and bolts of material for dress-making. Like milliners and jewellers, drapers crammed their windows with merchandise close up to the windows, and inside they always provided chairs at the counters. Large stores, such as Marshall and Snelgrove and Schofields of Leeds, had dignified floor walkers, and in their restaurants a trio to entertain their customers with music.

Book shops (except for W.H. Smith), sweet shops and toy shops were mostly private businesses. In the early years, the books of Beatrix Potter delighted children, as later did those of A.A. Milne. Many young people built up collections by buying Everyman, Collins, Nelson and other classics at 1s. or 2s. each. Novels in general in the 1930s cost 7s. 6d. Sweet shops, supplied by the famous local firms, ranged from those patronised by children buying the cheaper sweets to the specialist chocolate shops, selling chocolates by the pound or in boxes. As for toy shops, the German clockwork toys and the lead soldiers stocked before the First World War were remarkable. Everything was well-made – the magic lanterns with coloured slides, wooden jigsaw puzzles, elaborate theatres, delectable toy sweet shops, ingenious and substantial tricycles and pedal motor cars. There seems nothing of this quality today – except at a great price.

VICAR, VERGER AND DOCTOR

165
Vicar and verger. Rev J. Benson, vicar of Aysgarth (1949-1964), and R.W. Tunstall (1885-1969), who was verger at Aysgarth church for fifty years. He came in 1906 as gardener at the vicarage when the residing vicar, Rev D.H. Moore, had five indoor and three outdoor servants, and he served six vicars (1957).

166
Dr W. Alexander of Castle Farm, Castleton, North York Moors, who came from Northern Ireland in about 1860 and had a practice in Rosedale, High Farndale, Westerdale, Commondale and Fryup. He visited Rosedale on Fridays to attend to the large community of ironstone miners. His son, Dr Jack (d. 1949), although unqualified, practised with him, and they kept up to nine riding horses in a field opposite Castleton church (1900).

PROFESSIONS

167

Reginald Farrer (1880-1920) of
Ingleborough Hall, Clapham;
botanist, plant hunter, collector,
traveller and author who
popularised rock gardens. He was
converted to Buddhism in Ceylon
in 1907, and is here seen in
Buddhist costume.

168

The Leeds sculptor, E. Caldwell
Spruce, finishing the bust of Lord
Airedale presented to the City of
Leeds by Sir William Middlebrook
of Morley, and now in the city art
gallery. James Kitson, first Baron
Airedale (1835-1911), iron and
steel manufacturer, was a pioneer of
the engineering industry in the
north. (In 1912 the Hunslet works
making locomotives employed
2000 workmen.) Lord Airedale
was the first Lord Mayor of Leeds,
MP from 1892 to 1907, a Liberal,
a Unitarian and a philanthropist in
many spheres, notably housing,
pensions and education (1911).

169
J.B. Priestley (1894-1985)
dramatist, essayist, novelist and
critic pursuing his hobby of
painting at Ribblehead in his
favourite landscape of the
Yorkshire dales.

MOUSEMAN AND PHOTOGRAPHERS

170

Robert Thompson (1876-1955) the wood-worker or 'mouseman' of Kilburn, was the son of the village joiner and wheelwright who eventually established a furniture-making business of world-wide fame in his native place. In 1925, six men were working for him (soon to be increased to thirty) and churches, colleges, schools and some private houses and hotels all over the country were embellished by his work. His mouse symbol represents 'endeavour in quiet places'. Many of his apprentices have branched out on their own and have adopted their particular trade marks, and his own firm still flourishes (1934).

171

George Page had a clock and watchmaker's shop in Westgate, Guisborough. He was 6 feet 7 inches tall, and always had a parrot in his shop. Photography was his hobby, and he left many photographs of the period 1900 to 1910.

172

The photographer – Sydney Smith of Pickering (1884-1958) on Blue Bank near Whitby, 3 June, 1934. His photographs and equipment are to be seen at the Beck Isle Museum, Pickering.

CRAFTSMEN

173
Jet workers: John Barker and Joseph Gourley Lyth polishing in William Braithwaite's shop in Haggersgate, Whitby, in 1925. John was the last articled jet worker. Joseph, the last to serve the seven years' apprenticeship to the craft, was a famous polisher of jet, and latterly had a workshop of his own. He died in 1958.

174
The polishing shop of W. Waide & Sons, the Yorkshire Patent Churn Manufacturers, Leeds. Both barrel and end-over-end butter churns are shown (1890s).

175

Pitsaw in use at Bates saw yard, Huddersfield, in 1898. Before the introduction of mechanical saws, all boards were sawn by hand by a top and bottom sawyer in a saw pit. To speed on this monotonous work they used to recite rhymes such as 'Addle and tak't' to the rhythm of the sawing.

176

Spurr, shoemaker of Bramley, hand-sewing a boot. Shoemakers, or cordwainers as they were called, were always the most numerous of craftsmen. Following the mass production of shoes and boots, shoemaking ceased in general, but repairing continued.

177

Edgar Armstrong, blacksmith, who hailed from Malhamdale, lived at Arncliffe, Littondale, and is here shoeing a horse at Malham Smithy (date unknown).

STONE

178
A Swaledale smasher, Mr Calvert, breaking stones on the Buttertubs Pass for use on the roads (1920s).

179
John Hunter walling a gap on the Buttertubs Pass, Swaledale (1965).

180
Quarrymen, with the foreman wearing a bowler hat, in a quarry in Eskdale, where particularly fine sandstone was obtained (early twentieth century).

BAKING

181
Glazed earthenware baking bowls,
used when most people baked bread
at home, in the warehouse at
Lindley Moor Pottery, near
Huddersfield (1928).

182
Alfred Oldroyd, oatcake baker,
mixing dough for oatcakes at
Messrs Oldroyd brothers,
commercial oatcake bakers, High
Burton, near Huddersfield. There
were formerly many oatcake bakers
in the West Riding, but they have
all gone (1933).

WOMEN'S WORK

183
Mary Alderson making cheese at Angram, upper Swaledale.

184
Ella Metcalfe baking bread, teacakes and gingerbread in her kitchen at Croft House, Askrigg, Wensleydale (1950s).

185
Fireplace at the Wagon and Horses Inn, Saltersgate, on the Whitby to Pickering road. The hot air oven was cast by F.Dobson who had a foundry at Pickering, and it is heated by a separate fire beneath it to bake the turf cakes shown inside. There is no boiler; six kettles stand on, or near, the turf fire which was said never to go out (1930s).

DOMESTIC SERVICE

186
Domestic service used to be a widespread occupation for working-class women, often recruited at registry offices from the coalmining families of the West Riding and Durham. Mansions employed large staffs with a recognised hierarchy. Some middle class households might have three maids – a cook, housemaid and tweenie – others had one (the cook-general) supplemented by help from a charlady, but the toughest jobs were often on farms. Here, at Wetherby, Lucy, Dora and Clarice are respectively cook, char and general (early 1930s).

BONNETS

187
Staithes bonnet-makers, H. Anderson, P. Verrill and a friend. Formerly when out of doors all women wore bonnets.

188
Workshop interior at John Barran's, clothiers, Chorley Lane, Leeds, decorated for either the royal visit in 1908 or the coronation in 1911. The lighting is gas and some of the women wear bonnets. In the mid-nineteenth century, John Barran pioneered the clothing industry in Leeds which developed into an important trade with many firms employing thousands.

POSTMEN

189

John Rukin, farmer and postman of Keld, Swaledale. He is seen here at Tan Hill Inn which he at first visited three days a week and later he, or the Muker postman, went daily. In winter his route was via Crackpot Hall, East Stonesdale, round the village and Tan Hill. In summer he went across the moors on what is now the Pennine Way. He was a postman for thirty years from 1932.

190

Spurn Head postman, Mr Moore, and others, travelling on the sail-bogey on the Spurn light railway (1938).

191

The mail bus from Grassington leaving Buckden in Wharfedale about 1910.

ROAD MEN

192
Roadmen cutting snow with shovels just above Oughtershaw, upper Wharfedale on Fleet Moss Pass (1937).

193
Moving snow by shovel and manpower. Roadmen clearing the Kidstones Pass in 1937.

194

Wooden snow ploughs pulled by horses cleared snow from the roads. Harold Stead rides on the horse, and two roadmen, Frank Farrow and E. Barnett, follow behind in Appleton Lane, near Kirkbymoorside, 1938-9. They carried on until 1940.

195

Road tarring and gritting on Linton Lane near Wetherby in the 1930s. The hot tar was run off from the boiler, spread with wide brushes, covered with grit and rolled with a steam roller, seen at the back. Half the road is finished and the other half is being tarred.

CARTS

196
A Massarella ice cream cart in the Bentley area near Doncaster in the 1920s. They were well known for their canopies decorated with painted scenes. The Massarellas came from Setteffrati near Monte Cassino in Italy in about the 1880s and eventually, after selling ice-cream from a hand-cart at Doncaster, they developed a large business.

197
Children's roundabout on the Great North Road (the A1) in South Yorkshire. The owner with his roundabout and mule toured streets in colliery villages and in return for jam jars, gave free rides. The road is quiet with little traffic (1938).

198
David Burrow, carrier for thirty years between Sedbergh and Kendal with his horse, Spider, and spring cart, on the way to Kendal in 1930. He bought the business in 1910 from Kit Metcalfe and travelled three days a week, Tuesday, Thursday and Saturday, starting about 6 a.m. and taking some four hours. He took butter and eggs, collecting en route, and shopped for his customers. On Tuesdays, he only carried dyestuff for the drysalter, Isaac Braithwaite, to Farfield Mill, Sedbergh. Because of the steep hills, the cart took only about 10 cwt., and he charged 4d. a parcel up to 1930 when this rose to 6d., 9d., and 1s. He returned home about 6 p.m. David Burrow was 'the last carrier out of Kendal'.

ITINERANTS

199
John Wilkinson, known as Scouring Stone Johnny, who lived in Coverdale. On Roova Crags, he collected soft sandstone which he sold at a penny a piece on his rounds in the dales. He died in the 1920s.

200
Many packmen or Scotch drapers have, over the years, toured the dales selling drapery goods and haberdashery. James Cowley from Lancashire was the last to walk the rounds. Here he is in Littondale in June, 1937. He died later that year.

201
Gypsies making pegs for sale in the Huddersfield district.

202
Organ grinder and monkey,
probably near York (early twentieth
century).

203
Robert Allenby of
Heckmondwyke, a worker for
Moorhouses who had a fish shop
and hawked fish in the baskets
(early twentieth century).

204
Scissor and knife grinder in a street
near Bradford (early twentieth
century).

CAVE GUIDE AND INNKEEPER

205
Arnold Brown of Clapham, cave guide for Ingleborough Cave from 1939 to 1962, conducting a party of schoolboys holding candlesticks (early 1950s). It is on record that guides were hired in the eighteenth century to show visitors round the caves of Craven.

206
Alexander Pounder, innkeeper at Tan Hill Inn (1890s).

ODD JOBS

207
Steeplejacks repairing the chimney of Manningham Mills, Bradford, in the late 1930s. When the chimney was completed in November 1873, Samuel Cunliffe Lister, the architects and others ascended to the top and named it Lister's Pride. It is 94 yards high and cost about £10,000.

208
Harold and Artie Hodgson of Scarborough, who were chimney sweeps in the winter and donkey men on the sands of the North Side in summer (c.1913).

209
Newspaper boys in Leeds at the time of the relief of Ladysmith, 28 February, 1900.

SHOPS

210
James Street, Harrogate, in the 1930s. The shop on the left, Marshall and Snelgrove, was a high class department store and restaurant. The firm had branches in London, Leeds, Scarborough, Sheffield, Manchester, York and Bradford. They were once the shops *par excellence* for clothes for the middle classes, and are now no more. The doorman can be seen above the first car.

211
County Arcade, Leeds, built in 1898. Leeds had several arcades, of which some have gone, but this, an early indoor shopping precinct, remains. Smiths on the left was a well-known draper's shop, and tea could be enjoyed to the accompaniment of a small orchestra in Lyons café (early twentieth century).

212

Terry's shop and restaurant in St Helen's Square, York. It sold the famous Terry's chocolates, and the restaurant was a rendezvous for many visitors to York. Terry's catered for the children's parties of the district, and their ices are particularly remembered. When the shop and restaurant closed on 26 September 1980, members of the York Georgian society, dressed in mourning, had their last cup of tea there.

213

Parkinson's shop in the High Street, Doncaster, about 1905. S. Parkinson & Son, family grocer, tea dealers and confectioners, 50-51 High Street, makers of the famous Parkinson's Doncaster butterscotch, was founded in 1817. It is still there, but the butterscotch ceased to be made in the town a long time ago. Other Yorkshire specialities, named after towns, Harrogate toffee and Pontefract cakes, still flourish.

214

The first Marks and Spencer's shop to be opened outside Kirkgate Market, Leeds, where in 1884, Michael Marks had started trading. The Cross Arcade shop, Leeds, opened in 1904. It was still called the Original Penny Bazaar, and was closed in 1910. During the following years, shops were opened in Briggate and Leeds. When a new store, built in Briggate in 1939-40, remained incomplete, it was requisitioned for war purposes by the Ministry of Works, until in 1950, the new Marks and Spencer's store was completed and opened, and the old store closed (1904).

215

Interior of Lawrence's Old Chemist's Shop at Knaresborough. Established in 1720, it is reputed to be the oldest chemist's shop in England.

SHOPS AND MARKETS

216
Haberdashery stall in Kirkgate market, Bradford. Here, in little pew-like booths, a meal, such as pie and peas, could be had for very little.

217
Market Hall, Huddersfield (1890s). The covered markets of the West Riding towns are famous.

SHOPS

218
William Hannan's newsagent's shop established in 1891, 1 Butcher's Row, Wakefield. Newsboys in front (early twentieth century).

219
Six chimneys, Kirkgate, Wakefield, built in 1566, showing Bell's cooper's shop with dolly tubs and dolly sticks, barrels and a wooden pail. This building collapsed in 1941 (c.1900).

220

The mechanical model of
jet-workers, made by George
Wood, jet-worker of Whitby, in
1889. It has eight jet-workers at
their treadle wheels, chopping out,
turning, leading, finishing,
brushing, polishing, milling and
grinding, and by putting a penny in
the slot, realistic action was
simulated. The men's faces are
carved from old clay pipes. It used
to stand outside Elisha Walker's jet
shop in Church Street, Whitby, in
this century, and is now in Whitby
Museum.

221

Originally a blacksmith's shop, the
saddler's business was founded by
the Marshalls in 1863 on Penny
Hill, Hunslet. From left to right:
saddler, Jim Rider, who started up
in opposition, Albert Marshall, an
apprentice, and Albert's younger
brother, then about fourteen, who
ran away to sea, became captain of a
liner and ended up as harbour
master at Cape Town. Lastly, a
collar worker (1890s).

222

Samson C. Appleyard's grocery stores, opened about 1895, opposite the New Inn, Upper Town Street, Bramley. Samson's window came to be regarded as a work of art, and his tea was famous for its 'great strength and endurance' (1903).

223

A Christmas display at J. Mason's butcher's shop in Brook Street, Ilkley. Jim Mason and his wife stand in the doorway with Matthew Mason and an assistant alongside. The railway bridge has gone (1897).

224

Village shop. Betty Chapman in the newsagents, sweets and fancy goods shop in Askrigg, upper Wensleydale. Beginning in different premises in 1928, Betty and her husband, Azariah, followed by their daughter, Elizabeth, ran it for fifty years until the latter's retirement in 1978.

225

Miss D. Forrest and an assistant at Manchester House, Elland, which stocked all types of drapery and haberdashery goods – anything from a needle to bed linen. It was founded by Miss Forrest's father in 1900, the year of his daughter's birth, but it no longer exists in the same premises.

226
Throup's greengrocer's shop in the main street at Silsden, near Keighley (early twentieth century).

227
Pawnbroker's shop with three balls above, in Huddersfield. Before the days of social security, many pawnbroker's shops flourished in cities and towns. Cash was scarce, and they were a routine for those falling on hard times who acquired needful money by pawning goods at the beginning of the week and redeeming them again at the end. Jewellery, as seen in the window, was always traditional stock.

228
Martin Jeffery at the door of his tripe shop in New Road, Mytholmroyd, Calderdale. He also went round carrying a pea pan, with charcoal fire underneath, shouting 'Peas all hot'.

V

· *Transport* · *Leisure* ·

Early in the century horse transport was at full strength and the railways were going at full steam. Goods went by rail or canal rather than by road. Excursions by train were popular, and in holiday weeks, people went by train either to Blackpool in the west or to Scarborough in the east. Holidays with pay came in with the 1938 Act, and holidays for everyone, rather than the isolated feast, fair or Christmas days, arrived in this century.

Cycling and walking were encouraged by the Cyclists Touring Club, Youth Hostels (1930) and the Ramblers Association (1935). Bicycling brought the first sense of personal freedom for many, especially women, and the film 'A Day Out' by Alan Bennett, featuring a men's cycling club outing, ranks with that other classic film 'Night Mail', which follows mail sorting on a night express. Early in the century people went on walking tours, but by the late 1920s the term 'hiking' had been introduced, and we ourselves hiked to the dales and the Lake District. By then it cost 6s. or 7s. a day all in for rooms. Small hotels at 10s. or 12s. a day were considered expensive for walkers.

Above all, motor cars (at first for the privileged few), motor charabancs, coaches and lorries heralded immense change. In 1905 there were 16,000 private cars in the whole country and in 1950 2,258,000. In the early 1930s, forty miles an hour was regarded as fast – speeding drivers were called 'road hogs' – saloons had replaced open tourers and roads were peaceful. As a child, Joan Ingilby bicycled on the Great North Road because it was flat and quiet. Cars were cheap – an Austin 7 cost £156 in 1924 – and de-carbonised, could last for years. Early in the century, families with their women passengers swathed in veils against the dust drove to the Strid and Bolton Abbey or Aysgarth Falls, and in the 1920s, went on motor tours to Scotland or Devon and Cornwall. We lost something with horses which, although not free from accidents, could not go fast and had to be treated gently, but motorised transport has given infinite pleasure and opened up vast new possibilities.

133

We should like to have found a photograph of a family playing card games or singing at home around the piano – customs finished off by the wireless, gramophone and wider interests. Records of Caruso and Galli-Curci and the songs of Harry Lauder delighted many. Love of music is portrayed in the photographs of choral singing and brass bands, traditions which have survived the years with continuing popularity.

Over the years, theatres and cinemas have come and gone. In the 1920s and 30s, we ourselves saw the plays of Shaw and Barrie at the Grand Theatre at Leeds. Other productions attracted large audiences – Sir Frank Benson in Shakespeare, Sir John Martin-Harvey in 'The Only Way', Carl Rosa and the British National Opera Companies, the works of D'Oyly Carte, the musical comedies 'No No Nanette' and 'The Girl Friend', and the pantomimes for children at Christmas. Our period almost spans the rise and decline of the cinema, with many picture houses being built before 1914 and many demolished or turned into bingo halls in the 1950s. Numerous picture houses provided escapist entertainment for millions and major silent films accompanied by cinema organ recitals were occasions. We saw Charlie Chaplin, Rudolph Valentino, Gloria Swanson, the Gish sisters, Lon Chaney and Ivor Novello, and in 'Talkies' in the 1930s Clark Gable, Cary Grant, Greta Garbo and Marlene Dietrich, to mention only a few of the stars.

Almost in the same period, ballroom dancing with foxtrots, tangos and the Charleston became a craze. New dance halls attracted thousands, as did dinner dances at hotels and private balls. Again, the wireless and gramophone records brought the tunes played by famous jazz and dance bands into our homes. Those remote, carefree days were blotted out for a generation by the outbreak of the Second World War.

TRANSPORT

229

Jim Collins and his horse, Bonny, at Crofts Hill pump, Flamborough, which is still there but the pond has gone. Before the days of piped water in the villages of the chalk Wolds, water was in short supply, and it was fetched in water carts from pumps and ponds. At Flamborough, where there were four pumps, everyone owning a tub or water cart had to be a shareholder, paying 16s. plus ½d. for every load of water fetched from the pump (1920) (F. Brearley).

230

Members, horses and hounds of the Holderness Hunt crossing Wawne Ferry in the East Riding about 1908. The ferry across the River Hull ceased to function in the 1940s.

231

In 1898, the North Holderness Light Railway had been projected but it lapsed and to replace it, a motor omnibus service run by the North Eastern Railway Company was started in 1903, travelling from Beverley via Brandesburton to Driffield. These were the extraordinary-looking buses provided, seen near the Black Swan at Brandesburton. The service ceased in 1915.

YORK STATIONS

232

The old station at York seen from the Walls. It dates from 1840-2. Excursion trains left from here for Scarborough where there was an excursion platform. The huge Royal Station Hotel (now the Royal York Hotel) is seen on the left, close to the present York station (c.1916).

233

York Railway Station – no 4 platform (1914). The well-known curving shed was built in 1877.

RAILWAYS IN THE 1930s

234
A massive 0-8-0 goods locomotive
heads a long train of coal wagons
through Brighouse, on the Calder
Valley main line from Wakefield to
Manchester (c.1930).

235
An eastbound express passes the
castellated Woodhead station to
enter Yorkshire from Derbyshire,
1936. It is about to plunge into the
three-mile long Woodhead tunnel
(now closed) which took the main
Manchester-Sheffield line through
the Pennines.

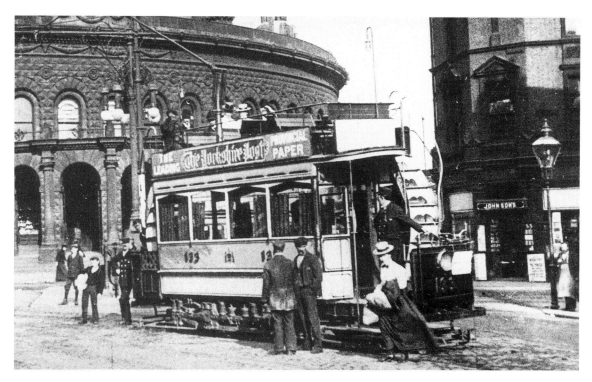

EARLY TRAMS

236
Open-top tram near the Corn Exchange, Leeds, (early twentieth century). Providing transport for towns and cities, trams were first drawn by horses in the 1880s, then steam driven and finally run by electricity with overhead cables. The clanging as they changed tracks and the ringing of bells to clear traffic was a familiar sound in town life.

237
Steam tram at Huddersfield.

MILL TRANSPORT

238

Early mill transport. Delivering bales of wool to a mill near Huddersfield. The men wear short 'brats' (overalls).

239

Lorries with bales of wool and a horse-drawn rulley with bags of tops in Cape Street, off Canal Road, Bradford in 1937. The building is the City of Bradford Conditioning House, built in 1902. It houses the organisation set up by Bradford Corporation to carry out quality control for the wool trade, in particular the moisture content of fibres, cloth strength, wear, fastness to light and so on. This unique institution still operates but is under threat.

KEEL AND BARGES

240
The classic Humber Keel on the River Ouse near Selby in 1938. It was rare at that time and is now no more except when specially preserved. They were used on the Humber, up the Ouse system and on the River Trent and varied in size according to the dimensions of the lock pits on each navigation.

241
King George Dock, Hull. Off-loading North American hard-grained wheat into a barge for transport to the mills on the River Hull for processing. This, and the one behind, belonged to Spillers, but there were also Ranks and other millers (1938).

242

A compartment boat train, 'Tom Puddings', entering Goole dock in 1949. This unique system was developed in the 1860s on the Aire and Calder Navigation to transport coal from the West Riding coal field to Goole. At its height, there were 1100 boats each holding forty tons of coal. A train consisted of up to nineteen compartment boats pulled by a tug, with a crew of four, which allowed 700 to 800 tons of coal to be moved. The system continued until July 1986.

243

The crowded scene of barges and tugs at Naburn Lock. Anything from cocoa to stone, grain, coal, manure, even gunpowder, needed in York used to go by water from Hull. Now there is only the occasional barge, usually for pleasure not freight (early 1930s).

HORSE AND DONKEY TRANSPORT

244
All the fun of an outing is expressed by this photograph of a party of visitors being driven along the road to Lastingham by Joseph Dowson of Kirkbymoorside in 1911. As they bowl along, dust rises round the wheels from the white limestone road.

245
Michael and Susan Peacock (1876-1937) on the near side, in Arkengarthdale after their wedding at Bowes church in 1910. It was Susan's second marriage, and she was at Tan Hill Inn for thirty-four years. The driver is Tom Guy, the best man Dick Scott, and the bridesmaid, Mary Rukin, with the vicar of Muker(?).

246
The miller's wagon from
Turnbull's, Sinnington Mill, on
Hutton Bank near Hutton-le-Hole
in 1933.

247
The Saltburn Corporation dust cart
pulled by a donkey called Jerry, a
great favourite (early twentieth
century).

LIGHTHOUSE AND LIFEBOAT

248
Outing from Bridlington to Flamborough Head and the lighthouse, about 1920. The charabanc has wooden artillery wheels.

249
Bridlington Corporation horses about to launch the lifeboat on the North Beach, turn of the century. When the maroons were fired, the eight-horse team, wherever they were in the town, were released from their traces and ridden to the lifeboat house. The horses were given extra rations, so the older animals were always keen to go when the rockets were fired. However, it could be dangerous and occasionally horses drowned.

EARLY TRANSPORT

250
Josiah and Jane Burnley and their son, Thomas Henry, of Morley on their motor bicycle and sidecar about 1909. Motor bicycles and sidecars were a popular form of transport and some families travelled many miles all over the country in them.

251
Semerwater frozen over in March 1919. The ice was thick enough to support an Austin 7, two motor bikes, and a group playing ice hockey.

OUTINGS

252

A botanical outing in 1913. The Hartley family (Marie is behind the windscreen) arriving in the car of a family friend, W.B. Stockwell of Morley, to find Dusky Cranesbill (*Geranium phaesum*) at Moreby Hall near York. The motor car is the 15 horsepower Armstrong Whitworth model, 1910-11.

253

Model T Ford ready for a wedding. It was used as a taxi by Percy Smith, a smallholder and farmer of Hutton-le-Hole who later converted it to a small lorry (1923).

254
Charabanc outing, Potter Hill,
Pickering (c. 1900).

255
Outing at Hebden Bridge in the
Calder Valley. Early charabanc
which belonged to 'Plonk'
Sutcliffe. The body was lifted off
by a crane and was used as a lorry
during the week (early 1920s?).

256
An outing to Kettlewell. A party of
businessmen from Ilkley, mostly
Bradford wool men, are resting
after a game of cricket. They had
come by wagonette, had lunch,
played cricket and returned after
enjoying a high tea (late 1890s).

257
A visit to Gordale Scar in the late
1890s. The ladies lived at Leeming
vicarage and must have travelled by
train to Bell Busk and by trap or
wagonette to Malham.

258

Many people have their favourite abbey ruin. We should perhaps plump for Bolton Priory as the most beautiful of the many monastic ruins in Yorkshire. The priory and its surroundings have been painted by Turner, Girtin and Cotman, and visited by Wordsworth and Ruskin. Owned by the Dukes of Devonshire, its woods were laid out with paths in the first half of the nineteenth century. It has been the foremost attraction in the county for outings by tourists arriving on horseback, by wagonette, train and motor car (1937).

259

The Cavendish Pavilion, refreshment rooms between Bolton Abbey and the Strid. The pavilion, like the Memorial on the road above it, was named after Lord Frederick Cavendish who was murdered in Ireland in 1882. Wagonettes used to meet trains at Bolton Abbey station, and many others came from Ilkley and Harrogate. Even in the 1930s two wagonettes waited for custom at Bolton Abbey, but once there were over fifty.

POPULAR RESORTS

260
The Dropping Well at
Knaresborough in 1915. Objects
such as gloves, sponges, shoes and
hats are strung along the face of the
cliff and are petrified by water
coming from springs saturated with
calcium sulphate. It is one of the
most anciently known and popular
natural phenomena in Yorkshire.

261
Visitors to Roche Abbey near
Doncaster in the early years of the
century before industry surrounded
it. Roche, one of the Cistercian
abbeys of Yorkshire, was founded
in 1147 supposedly on a site near a
rock crudely resembling the shape
of Christ on the cross.

262
Cow and Calf Rocks near Ilkley.
One of the several outcrops of rock
in Yorkshire popular for walks and
outings. Others are Almscliff Crag
near Otley and Brimham Rocks in
Nidderdale.

263
Visitors approaching the keep of
Scarborough Castle (early twentieth
century).

OCCASIONS

264
The visit of King George V and
Queen Mary to Batley in 1912.
They were received by the mayor,
David Stubley, and visited Bottoms
Mill. Only an inspector and two
policemen are in evidence.

265
The 131st summer meeting of the
Yorkshire Archaeological Society
visiting Castle Dykes, Well,
Tanfield, and Markenfield Hall
where a photograph was taken on
4 September, 1936.

266
A group on an outing sitting on the 'eye' of the White Horse at Kilburn on the Hambleton Hills. The famous White Horse was made in 1857 by John Hodgson, schoolmaster of Kilburn, with the help of his boys and the men of the village.

267
Carnival at Great Horton, near Bradford, on 24 June, 1905. A bevy of women cyclists leads the procession. When introduced in late Victorian times, cycling for women was regarded as immodest but by now it had become very popular.

PICNICS

268

Picnic on a botanical outing from Morley to Moreby Hall, near York in 1913. From left to right: G. Hartley, Marie, W.B. Stockwell, H. Hartley, Alan, daughter of host, A. Ashwell (the botanist).

269

A picnic in the fields at Town Head, Askrigg in 1891(?). The only man is Joseph T. Chapman whose wife, Mary Lizzie Chapman, is behind him in white. The occasion may be connected with their wedding which explains the wonderful hats.

270

Drinkings in the hay field in mid-Wensleydale. All the members of the family, young and old, have joined in. One sits on top of the hay on a sweep (early twentieth century).

271

A wagonette outing from Hexthorpe near Doncaster, organisation unknown, to Edlington wood on 8 July, 1905. The men played cricket and the children other games, and Mrs Robinson and Mrs Stevens cut up sandwiches. Hens forage for crumbs.

SHOWS

272
Roundabout and strength testing machine in the foreground in the market-place at Stokesley in Cleveland on 18 September 1947 at the time of the annual agricultural show.

273
Judging Dalesbred sheep at Kilnsey Show in Wharfedale. The show, started in 1897, has a fine setting and is an important event in the dales.

274
Dales ponies showing their paces at Muker Show, upper Swaledale, in 1932. The show started in 1893, and in the 1930s there were four open classes for horses and eight classes for local horses. The produce section included a prize for two oatcakes baked on a bakestone before the fire. The cattle were all Shorthorns and there were eight breeds of poultry.

FAIRS

275
Helter Skelter at Bridlington Fair held on High Green on or around 21 October, Charter Day. The charter for markets and fairs dates from 1200 (c.1920).

276
Lee Gap Fair at West Ardsley, between Batley and Morley, an ancient fair whose charter dates from the twelfth century. It once lasted for three weeks and three days, and during the nineteenth and early twentieth century was famous for horses (1938).

277
Hull Fair, whose charter dates from 1299, turned into the largest amusement fair in the north of England and is still held in October. The many sideshows exhibit the macabre taste of the times (c. 1910).

278
Leyburn Fair in October 1906. Leyburn supplanted Middleham as the market town for lower Wensleydale and was granted a charter for a market and fairs in 1684. There were once four annual fairs for cattle and sheep, now reduced to the May and October fairs. Swing boats and a basket stall occupy the foregound.

279
The Pace Egg play being rehearsed
by the senior boys of Calder Valley
High School in 1956. This is a
revival of a mummers' play once
performed all over Yorkshire and
indeed England.

280
The Plough Stots at Goathland in
January 1938. The revival of this
ancient custom, relic of a pagan
ritual to bless the sowing of the
corn, has been added to by sword
dances.

281
A Boon Day at the Methodist
Chapel at Keasden near Clapham.
Eight men are giving their services
for repair work to the building
(1960s). It has since been turned
into a house.

CUSTOMS

282

The planting of the Penny Hedge at Whitby on the morning of Ascension Eve in May, 1908. It is one of the most ancient customs of Yorkshire still performed, originating from the terms of land tenure for making the Horngarth, an enclosure for a deer park. Isaac Hutton, on the left, planted the so-called hedge for over fifty years. The next man, the bailiff of the manor, blows his horn and calls 'Out on ye! Out on ye!'

283

The annual ceremony taking place in June in Ripon to celebrate the return from exile of St Wilfred who rebuilt the first cathedral there in 669. He is impersonated by a local man who, riding a white horse, declares the fair in the market-place open and rides round the city (1906). Note the errand boys with baskets on their arms.

PAGEANTS

284
'The world has no such woful wight' – the Sherman's play from the York Cycle of Mystery Plays. The cycle was performed in the Middle Ages by the York guilds who each mounted a play and toured the streets in June. A shorter version of the cycle was performed at the first triennial York Festival in 1951 in the grounds of St Mary's Abbey, and those who saw it witnessed a revelation. This is the 1954 performance when Joseph O'Connor took the part of Christ.

285
Zulus in the Batley Pageant in 1907. Many schools took part, and the theme for Carlinghow Boys' School was 'South Africa', portrayed by floats, soldiers of the king, jack tars, Dutchmen, Boers, Chinese slaves, Zulus and early settlers. The event attracted a crowd of 20,000 and raised £261 for Batley and District Hospital.

286
Lieut-Colonel J.U.M. Ingilby and his wife, Marjorie, dressed as Sir William and Lady Ingilby who welcomed James I to Ripley Castle, near Harrogate, appearing in the historical pageant 'Ripley in Olden Days' at the castle in July, 1930. During the 1930s pageants were performed at several towns.

MUSIC IN THE WEST RIDING

287
Upper Slaithwaite Brass and Reed Band, formed in 1892, on a round at Christmas time outside Bradshaw Farm, Slaithwaite, Colne Valley (early twentieth century).

288
The band plays in Lister Park, Bradford (1920s).

289
The Huddersfield Choral Society
in Huddersfield Town Hall giving
a performance of 'Messiah' with the
BBC Northern Orchestra on 22
December, 1948. The conductor
was Malcolm Sargent and the
soloists were Isobel Baillie, Gladys
Ripley, Eric Greene and Norman
Walker.

290
Hebden Bridge Brass Band leading
a civic procession at Hangingroyd
on the way to Birchcliffe Chapel
(c.1914).

ENTERTAINMENT

291

The Bradford Alhambra from a programme for the week 31 January to 5 February, 1927. In that and the following week, fifteen operas were performed by the British National Opera Company. The Alhambra was built in 1914 as a music hall by Francis Laidler, and in 1922 became a multi-purpose theatre.

292

A programme cover of the Majestic (cinema) in City Square, Leeds. Opened in 1922, the Majestic was one of the finest cinemas in Yorkshire, and showed some of the best films. In November, 1922 *The Four Horsemen of the Apocalypse* starring Rudolph Valentino was followed by Charlie Chaplin's *Pay Day*. The Majestic had an organ played by Harry Davidson, and a restaurant with a band where luncheon could be had for 2s.6d., 'Tea Dansant' for 2s., dinner from 5s 6d. and supper was served from 9.30 p.m. A 'dainty' tea could be taken in the theatre for 9d. It closed in 1969 and became a bingo hall.

THE MAJESTIC

EUROPES MOST BEAUTIFUL CINEMA

City Square, LEEDS.

General Manager – LEONARD DENHAM

293

From 1910 to 1932 George Royle's Popular Company, the Fol-de-Rols, performed each evening in the Floral Hall in the Alexandra Gardens on the North Side, Scarborough. They had started as the first mixed pierrot troupe on the North Sands. Celebrities appeared at the Floral Hall on Sundays and in 1920, included such great names as Pavlova, Dame Nellie Melba, Karsavina, and Owen Nares (1922). (Owing to the structural repairs necessary, the Floral Hall was closed in 1987.)

294

George Sutton and his Arabians playing at the New Victoria Ballroom, Bradford (1930).

GAMES

295

The Yorkshire County Cricket Team in 1905. It includes some famous players. Back row: C.H. Grimshaw, W.H. Wilkinson, W. Rhodes, D. Hunter, H. Myers. Middle row: G.H. Hirst, the Hon F.S. Jackson, Lord Hawke (captain), Mr H. Wilkinson, J. Tunnicliffe, and in front, D. Denton and S. Haigh. These were the days of Gentlemen and Players. George Hirst and Wilfred Rhodes were all-round best cricketers in the country.

296

Farm men playing Duckstones at Grindale on the Burton Fleming road on the Wolds. Each player had a duck, a pebble or round stone, and the one who was 'it' put his duck on top of a large stone whilst the rest aimed at it with their ducks. They rushed to pick them up whilst 'it' tried to tick (touch) one of them before he reached home. He could only tick if his stone was still on the boulder. If ticked the player was then 'it'. The cry was 'Your ducks off.'

297

Herbert Sutcliffe 1894-1978 and Percy Holmes 1886-1971 at Scarborough Cricket Festival in the 1920s. They were famous opening batsmen for Yorkshire. In 1932 in a first wicket partnership against Essex they scored 555 runs. Sutcliffe also partnered Hobbs and on twenty-six occasions – fifteen times in test matches – scored three-figures, seven over 200.

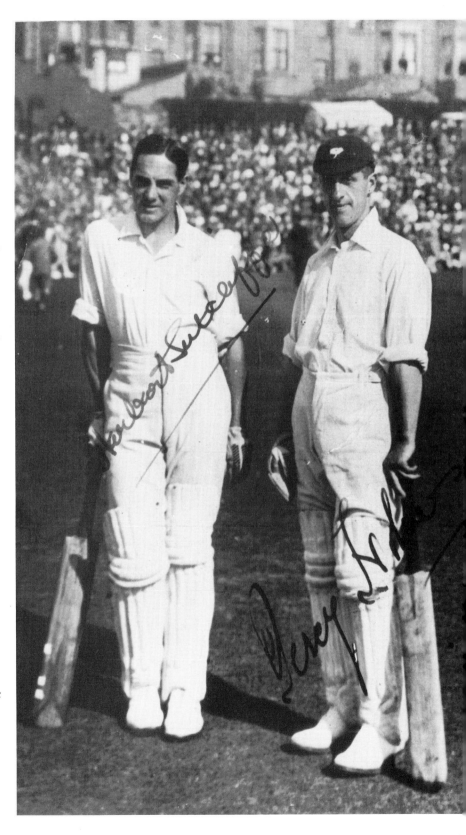

298
Men playing knur and spell in the
West Riding. There are several
allied games – piggy, tip-cat and
billets. Knur and spell may be
played with a trap which when
struck with the bat throws the ball
up into the air to be hit again as far
as possible, or with a sling with a
pot ball, as shown here. This game
was popular in the mining
communities in South Yorkshire
and was also played by lead-miners
in Swaledale.

299
Castle Bolton Feast, Wensleydale,
celebrated in September. A game of
quoits is in progress on the left and
a game of wallops (a kind of
skittles) on the right. Note the two
ling-thatched buildings (c.1910).

300
F.W. Spink of Easingwold with
his beehives on East Moors, above
Helmsley (1910-1912).

301
J.M.Hunt and Edwin Cook, then
aged sixteen with a 50lb. salmon
caught at Naburn Lock on the
River Ouse. Fishing for salmon
between Selby and Naburn Lock,
with drift nets manipulated from
the bank and small boats, used to be
general up to the 1940s. Usually a
catch was about three a day, sold to
dealers in Hull at 1s. a pound
(1936).

· Index ·